The Secrets Behind a Passionate and Loving Relationship

Andreas & Marie Skogvard

This book is dedicated to our precious daughters

Scarlet and Evolet

You have taught us so much about unconditional love.

We love you!

CONTENT

FOREWORD

Many of us carry the dream of a happy relationship or marriage. We long to find someone we can love, cherish and be with for the rest of our lives.

However, the challenge is to keep the love ablaze and sort out those conflicts that may surface. Therefore, love needs to be nourished, taken care of and valued. Love needs to be pursued anew day by day.

This book is written with the conviction that any relationship, and especially a marriage, is able to work well over time. Nevertheless, for a relationship to flourish, the couple needs to spend time with each other and focus on the more significant things in life.

A great couple relationship is characterized by certain basic traits in the same way that a great parent-child relationship is. The basic traits of a well-functioning relationship are **warmth**, **clarity** and **reliance.** You'll perceive warmth by the way love is expressed for each other through words and actions. Clarity is characterized by the set boundaries for faithfulness and for one another's personal space. **Reliance** means that words and action goes hand in hand. Reliance is built over time through great experiences together.

Love Ablaze gives, apart from great knowledge from different perspectives of a relationship, also a solution-focused viewpoint on the different issues that may arise in a relationship. After each chapter, there is a brilliant summary of the current topic. Moreover, they leave you with some points to ponder from each chapter as well. Reflections and an open conversation about the various topics are structured in a very good way to deepen and understand relationships and marriages better.

Some examples from the book:

Andreas & Marie write, *"All change begins with a decision."* This is so true. In any relationship it is obvious that decision-making is both a developing process where you try out different solutions on an issue, but it also means that you at one point just say, "Let's do it this way."

Another example from the book is that there is an emphasis placed on defining values and goals for the common future.

A prerequisite for a great future is the ability to share one's thoughts, make them clear and find common understanding.

It is of crucial value to learn to know one another deeply as this will greatly affect the development of both partners individually as well as the relationship itself. Our ability to show empathy and understand our partner's needs and wishes contributes to a large extent to the progress of that relationship. Moreover, a good self-knowledge plays another important role when it comes to a positive development.

This book is well balanced between the individual's needs and the responsibility you have in a relationship. *Love Ablaze* can in many ways make you happier together!

Dr. Sven-Erik Nilsson

Ph. D in Cognitive Psychology

Senior lecturer at a Swedish university for more than 30 years

Supervisor and teacher of teachers and psychologists

INTRODUCTION

We all have a longing for happiness and satisfaction, dreaming about a loving relationship filled with care, affection, intimacy, understanding and a sense of belonging. But why are so many couples not experiencing the dream of their life? Why is it that so many couples begin their love journey, travelling together on their road of romance, but end up crashing not many years after it all begun? Could it be that we live in a "throw-away culture", where it is more common to give up a relationship than try to save it, soon after a "defect" is discovered? Has it become a norm to exchange the relationship and upgrade it to a felt superior model once the road gets bumpy and problems arise? The fact is that many, maybe the majority, are struggling to have a strong and happy relationship. There may be a million and one reasons for that, but many times the bottom line could be one or both of these two:

A lack of knowledge: Have you heard the expression *"people are destroyed because of lack of knowledge?"* When you learn to drive, you need to take driving lessons, study theory and take exams before the driving license can be yours. But when you enter a relationship or marriage, more often than seldom, we have discovered that many individuals and couples have spent very little to no time to equip themselves for the journey ahead by reading books, joining courses or seminars about communication, the needs of men/women or how to build romance. As a result, many relationships crash due to the simple fact that there has been a lack of knowledge about what to expect in a relationship and how to solve common issues that arises.

A lack of investment: A happy and harmonious relationship is not about luck; it's a creative work that needs proficiency, practice and patience. There is a saying that goes, "whatever you sow you will reap." Investing time and that which is necessary to build a strong loving relationship will be seeds that you sow to build your future, and will sooner or later bring forth results. You will start reaping what you dreamt about. There is always a cause and effect of our actions. Investing in your relationship is crucial. By reading this book, you are investing your time and money in your relationship, and it will produce results when applied.

We believe that knowledge about and investment in the relationship, and the other person, are key factors to enhance your love life. All too often couples seek help way too late when the relationship is on the brink of crashing or has already crashed. Hence, we encourage you to focus on prevention rather than cure.

If you think about it, your life is really largely made up by the relationships you have. Relationships are what really matter in the end. Therefore, it is wise to invest time, especially in the one you love, because it can either move you forward or backward.

In this book, we seek to address many of the common relationship issues that may occur in life. You may find that some are applicable to you and some are not. Our aim is to provide solutions to the most common ones. Although we are aware of the complexity of certain relationship problems, we believe if you follow the advice given in this book, within a short period of time, the chance is great that you will start to see major improvement in your relationship and build something that stands the test of time. **Let's begin the journey to improve your relationship with the one you love, and let love come ablaze!**

CHAPTER 1

RESOLUTION

All Change begins with a Decision

Isn't it very true that in order for anyone or any relationship to experience a change, there must first be a *willingness* to change? If there is a willingness to change, to make a decision to do so will then be a lot easier. We often say, "If there is a will there is a way." Your relationship can positively improve to the extent you and your partner are willing to change that which is required. **One common reason people and their relationships don't change is because they haven't decided to.** And very often, the reason why they haven't decided to change is that they are not convinced or haven't realized that what they are doing is destructive for their relationship. One such important decision to change could be reading a book like this to gather information and knowledge to be able to take necessary actions for your love to come ablaze.

Our goal is for love to come ablaze, so in order for us to know that it has, we need to aim towards a greater understanding about love. Can true love be described in a simple way, although it seems so complex? At least we should try to get our hands around it so we know what we are aiming for.

I don't know about you but for me (Andreas), there was a time when I was wondering what love really was. I remember the very first time I was asked by the one I was dating (the one who later became my wife) whether I loved her. My reply to her was, "I don't know, because I am not sure what love is." Most girls probably would have ended that relationship there and then, but my wife is not like most girls; she is exceptional. The point here is that the answer was a very honest one, because I was not sure about what love really was. If you ask people what love is, you would probably get as many definitions of it as the number of people you are asking.

Now, since love is such an important word and topic, and definitely something we talk a lot about, especially in this book, we would like to try to give it some clarity and understanding.

DIFFERENT UNDERSTANDING AND DEFINITIONS OF LOVE

Perhaps you have given some thought to and wondered about what love really is, just like us. Can it be defined? Can it be understood? And can it really be felt? Just think about it, the topic has fascinated scientists, psychologists, historians and philosophers over centuries. Furthermore, numerous poems, books and thousands of songs have been written about it. People have killed for it, died for it and of course lived for it. **What is this phenomenon that expresses itself in so many varieties of ways?** When you look up the definition of love in most dictionaries, the meaning of love, as a noun, is most of the time described as **a strong feeling of affection**. But to be honest with you, that's a very simple definition of such a complex phenomenon as love. What we found out was, that according to some research, love could be psychological (some even claim that you love from your brain). It can also be physical as well as biological since there are many chemicals in the body involved. Others mean it's philosophical and some says it's spiritual; in other words, **love has been and still is extremely challenging to explain.**

One interesting research we found that we probably can use to grasp a little about love is from the expert on love, Dr. Helen Fisher[1], a human behavior researcher. Her sensational research has shown some very interesting discovery on romantic love. It shows that romantic love is a drive, and that it enables you to focus your energy on just one person at a time, one single individual. She claims that love is almost like hunger and thirst that you cannot be without. Her research about love also shows that romantic love has all the characteristics of an addiction. You focus on the person, you obsessively think about him/her, you crave the person, distort reality, and are willing to take enormous risks to win this person. Moreover, you want to see more and more of the person. **Romantic love according to Dr. Fisher is one of the most addictive substances on earth**.

Perhaps that's the reason why people look for it so much. There is a need for it, almost like an inbuilt craving, addiction or drive that you must get more of. Although Helen Fisher's way of explaining love is probably something most of us can identify with, especially when we are head over heels in love, most of us could also probably agree that there is more to it than that. The very famous passage from the Bible, which we so often quote during weddings, defines love in a very different way. It says:

"Love is very patient and kind, never jealous or envious, never boastful or proud, never haughty or selfish or rude. Love does not demand its' own way. It is not irritable or touchy. It does not hold grudges and will hardly even notice when others do it wrong. It is never glad about injustice, but rejoices whenever truth wins out. If you love someone, you will be loyal to him/her no matter what the cost. You will always believe in him, always expect the best of him, and always stand your ground in defending him."[2]

Here it seems like love is a lot more about being than a feeling or "addiction." Could it be that love is a combination of something that affects your entire being like an addiction or a "feeling" and something that expresses itself through actions towards others?

Although we only mentioned two different views of love here, there are many more. The way we would explain this complex phenomenon of love would be: **Love is something that affects your entire being**, something that affects you physically, psychologically, biologically and spiritually. It has the potential to influence your behavior like an addictive drive, which once tasted; you can't be without for a long period of time. You zealously think about that "one" person, having a longing for him/her, wanting to be together. You have a "feeling" that you can't get enough of the person nor live without him/her. This person is special and precious to you. The ultimate expression surfaces through your willingness to put his/her wellbeing and interest above your own; to be willing to benefit the one you love at the expense of yourself through words, actions and thoughts. Love is something you can choose to give away and direct passionately to someone, and you can also choose to receive it from someone.

FALLING IN AND FALLING OUT

What we did wonder about when reading about love was, if love is such a complex phenomenon, addictive in nature and unselfish in expression, is it then likely to just *"fall out of love"* and *"fall in love"* based on a feeling alone? Could there be more to it than falling in and falling out? We think we have arrived at the conclusion and the realization that it is more than randomly falling in and randomly falling out. It is mainly about a decision made to direct one's affection to someone specially chosen. So when someone says they have fallen out of love, they are basically saying they choose no longer to direct their affection/love to that person any longer. Of course, certain circumstances and incidents etc. may have affected that decision, but ultimately, a decision was made. Furthermore, how could you possibly stay in love for a longer period of time if it was just grounded and founded on a feeling? You couldn't. Everybody knows (who has been married or in a relationship for a longer period of time), that some days you feel in love and some days you don't. And those days when you don't, you have to rely on your commitment to that individual. Dr. Fisher also discovered in her research that the same part in the brain that is active when romantic love is experienced was still active in couples that said that they were still in love after 25 years of relationship. So let's talk about decisions.

LIFE IS FILLED WITH DECISION MAKING

Every day the average person will make thousands of choices. Even when you think you haven't chosen anything in a particular situation, you have, because you chose to refrain from choosing.

Someone said, ***"Decision is the bridge between your thoughts and your actions."***

When it comes to our relationships, we need to make many decisions, small and big ones. Some decisions are made on a daily basis and some are made only occasionally and can influence the entire course of our lives.

If we are honest with ourselves, we know that we are to a certain extent a product of the sum-total of the decisions we have made in the past. Regardless of where we are today and what our situation looks like, we can make a decision to let go of our past and not allow it to affect us any longer. We can choose to move on. In other words, when you make knowledgeable and informative decisions, you have the potential to change the outcome of your life and relationship.

Now, you may wonder what this has got to do with love coming ablaze? A lot my friend, because as mentioned earlier, **love is more than a feeling; it is also a choice we make**. We choose whom to love and how to express that love. We choose to whom we direct our affection. We choose how we will act and respond in the relationship, and whether we want to invest in it. And as we make certain choices, we can influence our relationship to come ablaze!

EVERY DECISION HAS A CONSEQUENCE

As you make decisions pertaining to you and your partner, you need to take into consideration *the consequences* of those decisions. If you don't agree or like the results of your decisions: change them.

Let's look at a simple example. You and your partner have a disagreement. You simply feel different about a particular issue and you can't understand your partner's point of view. You are getting more and more upset and begin to raise your voice to your partner. Instead of calming down and try to reason things out, you start to shout to your partner, walk out of the house, slamming the door after you, and refuse to speak at home for three days, giving him/her the silent treatment.

Here, you made a decision to let the feeling of anger control you. You chose to raise your voice, and you decided on the seemingly "easy way out" by leaving the discussion *and* your partner by walking out of the door. Furthermore, you refused to talk to him/her, despite several attempts from his/her side. A huge tension was built up at home, affecting the atmosphere as well as the emotional distance in between you both. Finally, you made the decision to break the silence and say that you are sorry, and you both reconciled. The point here is that the decisions made affected the outcome of the disagreement.

Now, could this situation have been handled in a better way? Could it have been conducted more lovingly and effectively, aiming to bring edification? The answer is yes, and this is where **it is of vital importance to reflect on what works well in your relationship and what doesn't**. If you and your partner over and again quarrel over the same issues or stumble over the same problems, it is advisable to see how a simple decision could change the outcome of not only the problem, but also the way you solve it. Ultimately, it will influence the quality of your relationship.

PLANNED DECISIONS

You and I need to make *planned* decisions: decisions that are made beforehand. You can call these planned decisions for your *core values* (read more about core values in chapter 8.) In this case, it could be how to act and react when disagreements happen, such as saying sorry quickly, or a motto such as "I love people the most when they deserve it the least because then they need it the most." It could be that you will never raise your voice to your partner, never argue in front of your children, or never use the silent treatment. These planned decisions will help you once feelings come and want to take away the logic reasoning in your actions.

Just like a flower needs consistent watering to grow, a love relationship needs the same. The issue here is often procrastination and excuses we make; and by that we make the decision *not* to change. We may give ourselves excuses due to reasons such as being inconvenient, proud, unwilling and too busy. But it is not good for anyone to be indecisive in life. "Maybe tomorrow" and "I will do it later; maybe next week" often doesn't happen at all. The fact is that we often delay because we think a task is too unpleasant or inconvenient.

YOUR FUTURE IS SHAPED BY YOUR DECISIONS

Since your future is shaped by your decisions, **start by deciding to be a conscious decision maker!** Don't live by vague dreams and indecisiveness, but make some solid decisions for your future and then commit to live after those decisions. **A loving relationship is one of the greatest blessings a person can have in life**, so making important decisions regarding it is a well-invested thing to do. You may have made wrong decisions in your past, but you can change the outcome of your future by making more informative and knowledgeable decisions today. How do you do that? You do it by acquiring more knowledge and gaining more information about a certain matter.

One of the most important decisions you will ever make in life is *whom* you choose as your life partner. It is critical to spend time on *irreversible decisions*, which means those decisions that are impossible or at least very difficult to change. Who you marry is such a decision. Even though quite a number of marriages end up in divorce, isn't it true that those who marry really want their marriage to last for a lifetime? Otherwise they wouldn't have gotten married in the first place. So one of the most essential decisions you will ever make in your life is whom you invite to be your life partner. Therefore, one should wisely spend ample time to find out whether the person you're dating is Mr. or Mrs. Right, as this will heavily impact and shape your future. We have seen many people change for the worse because of whom they choose to have a relationship with. We cannot escape the fact that the relationships we have shape us. You become like the people you live with, interact with and hang out with. It is so true that bad company corrupts good character. Have you ever wondered why parents are so concerned about their children ending up with the wrong company of friends? Therefore, make decisions wisely; it will impact you in a positive or negative way. You choose!

RESOLUTION IS THE PREREQUISITE FOR CHANGE

Whatever choices you make pertaining to your relationship, it always starts with a resolution. Resolution means you have determination – you make up your mind about something you want to change, and then you take steps towards fulfilling that resolution. Someone once said, ***"A goal without a plan is just a wish."*** Don't just dream about a more loving and passionate relationship – set goals and plan how to reach those goals. The fact is that you have already started since you hold this book in your hand.

POINTS TO PONDER

- People are destroyed because of a lack of knowledge.
- A happy and harmonious relationship is not built upon luck; it's created.
- Simply expressed: love is a combination of "feelings" and actions.
- Decision is the bridge between your thoughts and your actions.
- Every decision has a consequence just as an action has a reaction. Therefore, do not make a decision hastily or when you are out of your right state of mind or emotion.
- Spend enough time on the irreversible decisions.
- Change the outcome of your future by making right decisions today.
- Bad company corrupts good character.
- The relationship you choose will shape you.

CHAPTER 2

REST

Minimizing Conflict and Maximizing Peace

Is there any love relationship or marriage that has no disagreements? – We don't believe so. A significant factor in a lasting relationship is not the *absence* of conflict, but how the conflict is *managed*. **It is possible to "disagree lovingly."**

A hard faced Englishman was seated on a train between two ladies arguing about the window. One claimed that she would die of heatstroke if it stayed closed. The other said she would expire of pneumonia if it remained opened. The ladies called the conductor, who didn't know how to resolve the conflict. Finally, the gentleman spoke up. "First, open the window. That will kill one. Then close it. That will kill the other and we will have peace."

That may not be the best way to minimize conflict and maximize peace, and it's definitely not recommended. We may not literally kill our partners during or after a conflict but very often we kill the relationship and bring death into it, by our inability to handle and deal with it correctly.

Have you ever been angry, raised your voice, trying to explain yourself to get your partner to think the way you think? Or perhaps you withdrew, gave the silent treatment, and gave up the conversations as you felt there is no point since you can't win? Maybe you just gave in to complying to what your partner wanted and with that, suppressed your irritation about the topic you argued about? Does any of this sound familiar in how you deal with disagreements and conflicts in your relationship? What do you think about these ways of handling conflict? Does it make you feel better afterwards? Does it help your relationship to progress and does it bring you closer or further apart? Do you have to give up yourself and how you feel to keep a peaceful home environment?

Somehow we have learned a behavior in handling conflict and we think it should be carried out in a certain way, that the feeling of anger is uncontrollable and all it bring is negative. But that is not true. **Conflict doesn't have to be negative, if it is managed correctly**. As a matter of fact, it can serve as a catalyst for bringing change into your relationship.

In simple every-day language, conflicts may occur when you perceive that your goals and wants/desires are being hindered or obstructed by your partner. You feel that you cannot achieve them. Often, the bottom line of all conflict is about needs in one way or the other. We have a conflict because we need something. And so often, conflict starts because one or both partners are only focusing on doing whatever makes them happy.

MEN AND WOMEN ARE WIRED DIFFERENTLY

What is important to understand, especially during a conflict, is that men and women are very different in the way they are wired. They often think, speak and act as well as react very contrarily. Women are generally more emotionally driven *("you don't understand how I feel")* while men are more problem solvers *("tell me the problem and I come up with the solution.")* If you have this in mind, it will help you communicate on the right "frequency" so that the conflict can be solved more successfully. It can minimize conflict and maximize peace in your relationship, as you possess a greater understanding of each other and your differences. Furthermore, you may have different childhood backgrounds, coming from different cultures and educational levels. You might have different views on everything from money matters to politics, needs and wants, interests, personality traits, and expectations of the relationship. It is very likely that conflicts may occur for the simple reason that you are just different sexes and because of the diversity of personality and background.

Herein lies an important truth we need to apply: learning to **enjoy the similarities and at the same time appreciate the differences as complementing each other**. Both of you have strengths and weaknesses, similarities and differences. Do use whatever you have to build up each other and complement one another, instead of letting it become a cause of conflict and argument. What if something has already escalated into a conflict or heated argument? How you do you resolve that in the right way?

11 STEPS TO SOLVE CONFLICT

1. Evaluate Yourself

The first step we should take in solving a conflict is self-evaluation. We should be truthful with ourselves about our part in the conflict, our mistakes, our failures, our selfish desires. Ask yourself, why has the conflict occurred? Did I contribute anything for this conflict to arise? Are there selfish motives behind the conflict? Am I angry because my partner blocked some of my goals? If we have an attitude of grace when we are trying to solve a conflict, we will most likely succeed. Those statements like *"put yourself in another man's shoes"*, *"don't' look for the speck in your brothers eyes while having a plank in your own"*, and *"whatever you would like others do to you, do it to them"*, are certainly very profound and powerful statements once practiced. We all need to be aware of the fact that everyone can make mistakes and one day we would need the same grace ourselves.

2. Listen Attentively

For this to be effective, you need to pick a time when both of you have eaten and are relatively rested (we are aware that it may be hard if your child is waking up often). If you are in the midst of a heated argument/conflict, you can suggest to your partner that you both continue to discuss the issue after dinner or after the children are asleep.

To listen attentively is to regard your partner and his/her words as important. In other words, to listen attentively is to give attention to your partner; not only by physical hearing, but also by listening with interest to someone important that has something significant to say. How do you practically do that? Listen with your whole being: your ears, your eyes and your body. Your body language is very important. Don't fold your arms or get distracted by things in the room. **Be fully present**. Give your partner your full attention and time. Let him/her feel that you try to understand where he/she is coming from. Try to put yourself in your partner's shoes. And do not interrupt; instead, let your partner finish his/her sentence. **Try to hear the message "in between the lines" to gain understanding** about the other person's perspective, concerns, needs and wants.

I remember when we learnt this. We tried to talk in the bed before going to sleep, but the problem was that I (Andreas) was often falling asleep, being too tired to talk. This caused tension in our relationship as my wife felt I was not taking her seriously, when I didn't listen to what she had to say. We decided to change time and place for our "you and me time", and that improved the quality of our conversations a lot.

3. Respond Calmly

Take time to cool down. When it is your turn to speak, talk with a calm voice. Never scream or even raise your voice. Remember, you don't have to prove your point, win the argument or have the last say, but you are in it to solve the issue at hand as efficiently as possible. When you remain calm, the chance that your partner will really listen is much greater. **We have found that when we both respond in a calm manner to each other, the chance of a faster reconciliation is much greater.**

On top of that, if you have children and they hear you disagree, they will copy you and learn from your behavior, so if you respond by being defensive or raise your voice, your children will with huge probability respond in the same way sooner or later. It becomes a learned behavior. Like someone said, "Children don't do what we say; they do what we do." **We never need to raise our voices**, not to our partners nor our children. Why? Because raising our voices wouldn't help. It would only bring disrespect into the relationship, and it would with a high risk escalate and get worse with time. So take a deep breath and start responding calmly. If you aren't ready to respond yet, perhaps because you are really upset, ask your partner to revisit the conversation later, and **take a break for a while to collect your thoughts**. Beware of negative and critical thinking. Instead, try to focus on how to solve the problem. You may want to take a walk outside or have some solitude time in your bedroom, and then come back to your partner to continue your discussion.

4. Say "I" instead of "You"
Use expressions such as *"I feel this way…"* or *"I get irritated when…"* instead of *"you always make me feel…"* or *"you did…"* The possibility of your partner being more open to your feedback is greater, and it is easier for him/her to identify with how you feel.

Be careful to use the words "always" and "never" in the "wrong" context. Don't ever say things such as *"you never listen to me!"* Rather use words such as "sometimes" and "now and then." Beware of false accusations, exaggerations and generalizations.

5. Focus on the Problem; not the Person

Be focused on the problem or issue at hand as you discuss. Don't bring up old mistakes or unresolved problems from your past. Don't start a "blame game" with your partner. If it is in the past, you need to drop it and let it go. Do not become personal and start to attack one another's character. Come from the point that you would want to improve a certain situation or solve a particular problem instead of accusing your partner for being wrong, attacking his/her personality or pointing out his/her weak points. Focus on the behavior; not the person. **The aim is not to put down one another but to improve the relationship. You are a team, solving a problem together.** Imagine yourself being on the same side of the table, tackling the problem on the opposite side.

6. Remember: You don't have to Win or get Even

Many times, you would need to find a common solution to a problem; especially when it comes to things that concern you both, such as how to raise your children, where to go for holiday or how much money you would want to spend on mum's birthday. Try to find a "middle road", or just let your partner decide if it is not a big deal to you. For many issues, it is OK to have different opinions and ideas. You just think differently and you don't need to feel the same way. Just remember to practice humility and selflessness. Remember, **it is not about winning a conversation that matters; it is about winning a relationship and solving a problem. Think as a team and you will be like a team**. Team players don't play *against* each other but *with* one another for a common goal.

7. Timeout

During crucial moments of a basketball game, the coach will call for a timeout. Very often, the reason for it would be to interrupt a "negative flow" for the team or a positive one for the competitors. Timeout during a conflict is the same. You would want to interrupt the emotional state you are in. It may sound contradictory at first, but it is not. **If your emotions are getting overheated, it is**

better to take a timeout and walk away. Either you decide to discuss this at a later stage (you can even agree on a time), or you go out for a short walk and calm yourself down and come back to continue your conversation. It is going to be close to impossible to solve a conflict if you are too emotional during the conversation. If you do seek timeout, keep your thoughts in control. Don't begin to curse, nurse or rehearse the disagreement, but disperse it and think about how to reverse it and find a solution.

8. Maintain Respect for your Partner

Avoid name-calling and never use the "D-word" (Divorce), which will only cause damage to your relationship. **Criticizing your partner harshly is actually attacking and sabotaging yourself, since you are a team**. Make a choice to remain respectful to your partner and explore various solutions to resolve the conflict in the most optimal way. One aspect of respecting your partner is to **never discuss conflicting issues when children are present, nor speak negatively about your partner to your children**. You display respect for your partner when you praise him/her in front of your children. It is also crucial to protect your partner in conversations with other people, whether he/she is present or not. **Respect starts in the mind**, so begin to think positive and uplifting thoughts about your partner (even though no one is perfect), and furthermore, **don't say anything *about* your partner that you can't say *to* him/her directly.** As you choose your thoughts about your partner, it will ultimately affect the way you feel about and treat him/her. Sometimes it takes practice to focus on the positive and to say good things, but once it is a habit, it becomes natural.

9. Say *"I am sorry"*

A wonderful way to honor your partner is to take the first step to reconcile. This is the most important tip we can give you when it comes to disagreements, and **one of the most important overall principles for a successful relationship**. To genuinely say that you are sorry will require humility. This means that you have to "swallow your pride"; otherwise your pride will get in the way every time in your relationship. Remember *the golden rule*: **do to others whatever you would like them to do to you**. So treat others the way you would want to be treated.

It is important *when*, *why* and *how* you say sorry. Three simple rules: Say it quickly, say it genuinely and say it lovingly. Someone once said: **"he who forgives ends the quarrel."** This is very true. Genuine regret and forgiveness softens the heart, ends the quarrel and brings the couple closer to one another. **Sincere forgiveness is unconditional**. When there has been repeated hurt in a relationship, it may take time to rebuild the trust in the relationship. But to use these three words often: "I am sorry", and really mean them, is a very powerful ingredient to stay happy in your relationship. Once forgiven, throw it into "the sea of forgetfulness," and never bring it up to the surface again.

Mother Teresa, a Catholic nun who gave her life to the poorest of the poor in the slums of Calcutta, once said: ***If we really want to love, we must learn how to forgive.***[3] You cannot build any relationship on bitterness, anger or criticism. To live a life where it is easy to admit wrongdoings and ask for forgiveness is very important if you desire a loving relationship. **Forgiveness is freedom**.

What some people have said about forgiveness

"Forgiveness is not an occasional act, it is a constant attitude." - Martin Luther King Jr.

"A good marriage is the union of two forgivers." - Ruth Bell Graham.

"Forgiveness is a lifestyle of being loving and gracious to others, even when they least deserve it, knowing that they need it and that you will need it yourself one day." – Marie Skogvard.

10. Settle Disagreements before going to bed
Irritation and anger will remain and intensify unless dealt with. It is always good to settle disagreements as soon as possible; after both of you calmed down and are ready to talk about the matter and how to solve it. See an unsettled disagreement as a cancer cell – unless it is dealt with, it grows and causes more harm. A good "rule": don't **let the sun go down on your rage**. That means to settle any disagreement before you sleep at night. With that, you will not hold grudges for days or have a "silent war zone" at home, where none of you talk to each other for long periods of time. Discuss what works for you both and then stick to it, no matter what. **Love needs guidelines and boundaries to stay strong**.

The last step to solve conflicts is:

11. Make Restitution
Someone once said, *"A good apology has three parts"*:

a. *"I'm sorry"* (Expressing regret)

b. *"It's my fault"* (Taking responsibility)

c. *"What can I do to make it right?"* (Making restitution)."

The problem is that many people forget about number 3. This is what we call making restitution. **Your aim is to make it up to the other person, to compensate for the damage, harm or loss that have been made**. Restitution seeks to restore and repair, whenever possible. It could be to be "overly accountable" or to be extra unselfish for a period of time, to prove one's love and allow the rebuilding of trust. **Don't make restitution actions in the way *you* feel is best**, but ask your partner how you can make it up to him/her. And remember to let things take some time. If there was deep or prolonged hurt, it may take time to heal and restore.

Our attitude determines our altitude. If your attitude towards your partner is positive, respectful and loving, most likely your relationship will also be positive, respectful and loving, and as such, the relationship will bring you and your partner much happiness.

THE BATTLE

A Native American tale tells the following: *A grandfather sat with his young grandson on a huge rock overlooking the lush valley below. "Sometimes when I think about people who have hurt me," the grandfather said, "I feel like I have a battle going on inside me." "What kind of a battle?" asked the grandson, turning to look at his grandfather. "It's a battle between two wolves. One wolf is kind and accepting and wants to live in harmony with all those around him. The other wolf is angry and fearful and wants to blame others for what has happened to him." His grandson, listening with rapt attention, softly asked, "Which one is going to win, Grandfather?" The grandfather gave a slight smile and looking down at his beloved grandson he said, "The one I feed, dear child. The one I feed."*

We all know it is always better to be proactive than reactive. So if you would like to avoid or minimize conflict in your relationship, do consider discussing and practicing these preventive measures beforehand:

DISCUSS AND PRACTICE REGULAR "YOU AND ME TIME"

At its most simple level, to avoid that a conflict occurs and/or escalates, set aside time to discuss when you have different opinions, frictions or disagreements. Have regular "you and me time" when you talk and discuss about things that concern you both and then try to find solutions together. If you have children, this is the time to tell your children that mum and dad need some time of their own (e.g. 15 minutes) without being interrupted. You may also have this "you and me time" after the kids have gone to bed.

An excellent couple will continually work on their relationship to tear down every wall that separates them, and in order to do that, regular time together with a purpose to share what's on your hearts is of crucial value. We advise you to have this "you and me time" at least a few times a week. Regular "you and me time" isn't only for the purpose of minimizing conflict, but it is also for you to **connect on purpose with your partner**. Just letting your relationship drift and hoping for the best won't get you anywhere. Connect on purpose. You can ask how your partner is doing and share what is in your heart. It will deepen your relationship and understanding for one another.

DISCUSS ABOUT FINANCES

One of the top areas of potential conflict to address is the financial area. If you live together, you have to work this out, because **the way you handle money will matter!** Issues about finances often cause stress and conflicts in relationships.

"Arguments about money are by far the top predictor of divorce," said Sonya Britt, assistant professor of family studies and human services as well as program director of personal financial planning[4]. *"It's not children, sex, in-laws or anything else. It's money for both men and women."* Sonya Britt even said, *"In the study, we controlled for income, debt and net worth. Results revealed it didn't matter how much you made or how much you were worth. Arguments about money are the top predictor for divorce because it happens at all levels."* So frankly, it doesn't matter how much you make. Financial arguments are not income-based. They affect everyone. It really doesn't matter how great your income is; poor couples and rich couples alike do quarrel about money.

What is the right way of handling money in a relationship? What is mine, yours and ours? Let us begin by saying that it depends on the depth and type of relationship you have. If you are married, should you put both of your income into one joint account, or should you maintain two totally independent accounts, or should you maintain two independent and start one common household account? These might be questions you have to ask yourself if you are going for a serious, committed relationship, living together and creating a future life together. The most common problems when it comes to finances that we have encountered in our work among couples are the following combinations:

The "Saver" vs. the "Spender." When a couple consists of this combination: one enjoys spending big sums of money and the other is very careful and wants to save most of it, they often work against each other by trying to change the other person. This causes tensions and conflicts.

Solution: Try to work out a "middle road" and agree on a common budget for your shared expenses and savings. Thereafter, you can spend the amount or save what you prefer with "your" money. Go back to your common financial goals for your relationship. If the spending doesn't interfere with your financial goals (see more in chapter 8), by all means, you can spend.

The "Hardworker" vs. the "Lazer." When one party works really hard and aim to succeed in his/her career and the other just lazes around, tension can become a fact. Working very little or not being willing to actively look for a job or creating a source of income will likely cause disagreements and pressure pertaining to finances.

Solution: The way you decide to deal with this issue depends largely on you as a couple and what you have agreed on in your relationship beforehand. Most people would agree on the fact that both parties in a relationship should contribute to the common household expenses, unless other arrangements have been made (for example a home staying parent). If it's for a short period of time, when one or the other is in between jobs or are looking actively to find one, the tension usually does not build up. If your partner is lazy, and shows no interest in finding a job to help you provide for all the expenses, even though you have brought it up on several occasions, you should come to a place where you put demands on you partner, a deadline with certain consequences. The question will always be how long are you willing to "support" your partner before it's enough?

The "Planner" vs. the "Impulser." The "Planner" will both save and spend but very carefully consider what he/she needs to purchase before buying it. The "Impulser" will just buy whatever feels good on the spur of the moment, pretty much like shopaholics.

Solution: Discuss through what is acceptable for both of you (depending on what kind of account set up you choose). For smaller and cheaper purchases, it may be OK that one is a "Planner" and one is an "Impulser" but probably not when it comes to buying a car or other expensive items. Once again, the key word here is to find agreement with one another.

When it comes to finances, our most important advice for couples is transparency. A poll by CreditCards.com suggests that as many as 7,2 million Americans are hiding money from their spouses.[5] It only tells us one thing – there is no trust in those relationships!

WHAT ARE THE SOLUTIONS TO MINIMIZE FINANCIAL CONFLICT?

Regularly talk about your finances. Unless you communicate and are transparent about this topic, it will sooner or later become a source of argument. Once you begin to discuss your spending and financial plans, it eradicates the edge of it.

Both should be involved in the planning and execution of your financial strategy. Although it's common that one of the partners in a relationship takes the main responsibility, it's advisable that you both are involved in planning your financial goals. Managing household economics is for both parties in a relationship.

Make a budget and stick to it. If you are going to avoid conflicts in your relationship, we advise you to sit down and make a budget. With an agreed budget, you both have to align to agreed investments, savings, spending etc. for the benefit of both. A budget helps you to see where your money goes and where you may be overspending. Many couples have little or no clue about how much they spend if you break it down to food, petrol, children, school fees and so on. However, it is advisable to frequently communicate about your budget and make regular adjustments to it to maintain a good and healthy financial future together.

Get a financial planner. We advise you to contact a financial planner to help you to structure your finances and set up a plan for the future. It will help you get things into perspective. At the same time, it will help you to plan and follow your agreed budget in order for you to achieve what you desire. As a couple, you frequently need to ask yourselves what you would like to achieve or accomplish and then plan for it. For example, if you one day would like to live in a landed property, you might have to set up a saving plan/investment plan to be able to achieve it.

Being a couple is a great financial advantage (if you choose a common type of account setup). You will have double income and can reach your goals much faster than if you do it alone. Research has shown that couples that talk about money every week are happier than couples that don't. [6]

The next preventive measure is for those with young children. If you don't have any, you can move on to RELATIONSHIP BUILDERS further down in this chapter.

DISCUSS SOLVING COMMON CHALLENGES WHEN YOU HAVE YOUNG CHILDREN

One of the most challenging times ever in many couples' lives is the time when they have young children. **This is the time when life often feels very intense and rushed, especially if both of you as parents are working outside the home, with demands on you to perform.** The continuous house chores of cleaning, cooking and doing laundry, have now multiplied with things like feeding, bathing, comforting, cuddling, playing, dressing, and caring for your children. All these tasks that so often need immediate attention (such as a filled diaper) can make you so occupied that you almost forget to "see" and furthermore, meet the needs of your partner. If on top of that you face other challenges such as babies waking up at night, colic issues, seriously ill children, or children with special needs, it can have a more serious negative impact on you as parents. It is especially common for the man to feel that his woman doesn't give him any attention or sexual intimacy, but that she gives all her time to the children. It is also common that the woman feels she does "everything" at home, and that she is the one that settles the kids "by default." **These situations often cause tension and conflict in the relationship, and if it's not dealt with, it might just escalate and "explode."** So what do you do if you are in this situation and you feel overwhelmed by all the things to do while the irritation and "gap" in between the two of you is growing? Below are a few practical tips that can have an immediate effect.

PRACTICAL SOLUTIONS TO PARENTS WITH YOUNG CHILDREN

The bottom line is always to communicate how you feel, what you need and what you wish for. **Both men and women need to speak up and have conversations about how to best solve issues that arise.** Here are some practical tips for parents with small kids that can help your everyday feel a little bit easier.

Write a list of daily chores on the fridge, and switch responsibilities every week. This helps you so you don't need to have any discussion about who is doing what, but you decide *beforehand*. This is a typical "planned decision" we discussed earlier. It applies especially to couples where both parties work an equal amount of time outside the home. In today's society, when both parties often work full time and have equally much to do, we advise you to share responsibility, unless something else has been agreed on and talked through. It can involve responsibilities such as cooking, doing the dishes, cleaning, fetching to school and putting children to bed.

Discuss parenting methods and aim to find common ones. It is not easy for "mom" and "dad" to use the exact same methods for everything when they raise their kids. What one parent allows, the other may not be agreeable to. However, **try to find as much consistency and agreement as possible**. Before babies are born, do discuss which methods you would want to use when it comes to matters like sleeping, feeding and tantrums. Common questions to discuss could be:

- Is baby going to sleep in your bed or in a crib?

- Is baby allowed to use pacifier and how much?

- How do you deal with baby crying?

- How do you deal with a toddler throwing tantrums?

- What kind of disciplinary methods will you use?

The more you discuss before your children come along, the easier it will be. Your views will likely change and alter when the baby is born, but you may want to have some foundation to start from. You can't prepare for everything, but as and when things come up, do sit down and discuss what will work best for your family. **Make adjustments when necessary and try to be con-**

sistent. You should aim to be in agreement as much as possible regarding your children's upbringing. If not, it can become a reoccurring issue, causing conflict again and again. Remember, as every child has a unique personality, there are certain methods and ways that might work with one personality but doesn't work with another. We had to deal with our two children very differently, as their personalities are so different, but yet beautiful in their own ways.

Let the other parent deal with the consequences of his/her parenting method. If you both disagree on certain methods, try to find a middle way. But if you still use different ways in some areas, let the other deal with the consequences of his/her method. If one parent allows the child to nap at 4:30 p.m. in the afternoon, then the same parent should be the one trying to settle the child at night, which would probably take much more time than if the child had his/her nap earlier in the day. **Never disagree in front of the children**. Support what the other spouse decides and talk after the children have fallen asleep.

Create "family rules." When your children grow a little bigger, you will find that more "rules" may need to be set. It could be things like washing hands before and after every meal or cleaning up the toys before going to bed. **Involve your children in house chores from a young age**. A two-year old can for example help with easier chores like putting back a few toys with your help, and a six-year old can set the table for dinner. It will take much more time when they help out, and it may not be the way you want it done, but you set a pattern for them to follow and it teaches them to be helpful. Moreover, it will help you in the long run as your children won't take things for granted, but the burden lightens for everyone when all family members help out around the house. You can set up a few rules on the wall with pictures so that everyone can understand. After a while, it becomes routine.

Seek the help of pediatricians, psychologists and/or other ex-perienced parents. If you have a child with special needs or a child that is sick, extremely active or doesn't sleep much, do seek professional help as how to best deal with the situation. When a baby or toddler doesn't sleep well at night for a prolonged period of time (some children doesn't learn how to sleep well by them-selves until they are two or three years old, or even older), it eas-ily becomes a stress and a reason why many parents wake up ex-hausted and have no energy to be nice to each other or their kids. There may be no easy solutions for these kinds of problems, but by talking to professionals or other parents, you may find solutions about how to soothe your child or get some tips how to deal with it, such as parents sleeping in different rooms alternate nights. If your child has a lifelong sickness or special need, you need more long term plans. One of them is to create a support system around you.

Find a support system. When you have children that may de-mand more of you, your time and energy, for example a child with autism or a physical disability, it is strongly advisable to create a support system around you. Ask parents or relatives to help you out, or put an ad in the local newspaper to source for a nanny or babysitter. Or you can consider letting your child stay with his/her grandparents one weekend a month so that you can focus on your relationship with your partner and/or with other children in the family. People may be more willing to help than you think. You often just need to ask.

Make time for intimacy. Many couples with young children find that their closeness to each other decreases, and that their sexual relationship is almost equal to zero after they have their first baby. Tiredness and busyness can make both parties temporary dis-interested in both physical affection and sex. You may think that there is no time, but you just have to make time. **The truth is that we make room for things that are important to us**. Intimacy with your partner should be of high priority, no matter what season you are in. Three practical tips:

Have regular "you and me time." As mentioned earlier. We advise you to spend about 15 minutes every day to connect with your partner. It should be a childfree time, and there should be no distractions such as TV or mobile devices. The purpose is to talk about the day and how you both are doing. You can for example have conversation over a cup of tea around the kitchen table.

Make the parents' bedroom a baby-free room at bedtime. Some couples prefer co-sleeping with the baby, and that is of course up to each one to decide, but one negative effect is that you may have very little time for sexual intimacy with your baby or child around. If your baby has fallen asleep in your room and you have the luxury of several other rooms, you can prepare one of the other rooms to go to once baby is sleeping, to have your "private couple's time."

Invest time in regular dating. It is good if dating occurs perpetually throughout life. Hire a babysitter or leave your child to someone you know while you and your partner spend an evening on a date with each other. You could perhaps set aside one evening a month as a start.

Set clear boundaries. You may need to have clear boundaries when it comes to grandparents or friends visiting, especially if the culture you stay in usually allows that anyone could just come and visit you in your home. Due to the intensity in your life, especially if you have more than one young child, parents need to learn to say no to certain events or dinners, or having people visiting too frequently. It is OK to say no or to leave earlier from a party or dinner because you have young children or you yourselves are tired. For a season, you have to do what is necessary for you to be able to maintain a great relationship and learn to feel comfortable with it.

Deal properly with interfering in-laws. Bear in mind not to take side with the parenting opinions of your in-laws or parents. If you've agreed to stay united in your parenting convictions as a couple, there won't be any conflicts over this matter in between you and your partner. Especially mother in laws have a tendency to want to have a say in the way you raise your children, and may impose their own upbringing methods on you. Be clear with your parents/in-laws that this is now your family. **You can listen to advice, but you have the final say in the matters pertaining raising your own children**.

Give each other "scheduled space." It is of crucial value to give each other some space, or what we also call "me-time." It can be as simple as giving each other one or two evenings "off" every week, off from cooking, putting the children to bed etc. At that night, one is free to do whatever he/she likes, for example exercise, resting, reading or meeting friends. If it is very hectic around dinnertime, you can consider having your "me-time" after dinner is settled. Another advice is to take turn to sleep in on weekends, such as one of you sleeping in on Saturdays and the other on Sundays, or alternate weekends if that suits you better. As you give each other scheduled space, you will likely feel that your motivation and energy level rises, and with that, your overall sense of contentment with yourself and your relationship increases.

Take control over your schedule. In the season when a couple has children in school age, life can be very hectic due to happenings such as school events, homework and recreational activities. For example, your son is playing soccer twice a week. You may need to fetch him for practice and games, and you might need to be involved in parent's support activities for that sports club. On top of that, your son also has piano lessons and basketball training. It can be quite tiring if your child has many activities after school, especially if you have more than one child. Hence, for the coming semester, why don't you consider letting your son choose one or two recreational activities? He can choose which one he would like to focus on. You can also check with other parents whether you can car-pool alternate weeks, or maybe you can come up with other creative ideas to ease your busy schedule. If you have younger children, bear in mind the involvement for both child and parents when you sign him/her up for new recreational activities. You can be in control of your schedule, and with that, you will find a balance in life for yourself, your partner *and* your children.

Whether you have young children or not, you would want to aim to **minimize conflict and maximize peace** in your home.

CREATING A PEACEFUL HOME

As it may not be possible to have a home totally free from disagreement and conflict, a couple can create a home where there is peace and where disagreements are discussed respectfully and peacefully. If both parties maintain a respectful, loving and unselfish attitude towards one another, you can still live happily in love with each other and the chances are great that you both will enjoy being at home because there is minimal conflict and maximum peace present. And who doesn't want that? If you already have disagreements and conflicts in your home, you can do something about it and solve it. Remember that getting your **love ablaze** is the goal.

RELATIONSHIP BUILDERS:

1. Practice speaking in terms of *"I"* instead of *"you"* in your conversations. Be conscious about the words you are using. Avoid "always" and "never" in the wrong context.

2. Decide and plan on starting to have a regular "you and me time." Do it on purpose.

3. Write down a list of house chores you need to do and discuss how you both can share the responsibilities. You can also do it together and use it as a couple's time.

4. Tell your partner something that you are sorry for. It may be something that happened during the week, such as something you said or did, or something you neglected to do. If you had a peaceful week with no matters to settle, think of something in the past that you have not asked for forgiveness for. If it is already settled – that's good! It probably means you have already built in this important ingredient of forgiveness in your relationship!

5. Think through whether there is any area where you need to make restitution. Consider discussing it with your partner and then start to do it!

POINTS TO PONDER

- How can anyone walk together in unity unless they agree? It's advisable to arrive at an agreement even if you disagree lovingly.
- Every great couple will continually work on their relationship to tear down every wall that separates them and unite every part that divides.
- Building a relationship demands shared responsibilities in the life lived together.
- Maintain a good intimate sex life even during the season when you have small children.
- Be careful to use the words "always" and "never" in the "wrong" context.
- When you discuss your relationship, learn to say *"I"* instead of *"You"*. (*"I feel hurt..."* instead of *"You hurt me."*)
- Words eventually become actions.
- Criticizing your partner is actually sabotaging for yourself since you are playing on the same team.
- Respect begins in the mind.
- Settle disagreements before you go to sleep; never let the sun go down on your wrath.
- If we really want to love, we must learn how to forgive.
- Three simple rules how to say sorry: say it quickly, say it genuinely, and say it lovingly.
- He who forgives ends the quarrel.
- Don't curse it, don't nurse it, don't rehearse it, but disperse it and reverse it.

CHAPTER 3

RESPECT

How to Communicate Effectively with Great Results

If you desire to build a loving relationship and are aiming for your **love to come ablaze**, respect is a vital ingredient. Giving respect to your partner as a valuable person with valuable inputs and ideas builds for the future. The opposite is also true. If there is no respect in attitudes, words or behaviors, the relationship will likely sooner or later end. Very often it can help to look at the opposite of respect to understand what it is. Try to avoid these disrespectful behaviors:

FOUR DISRESPECTFUL BEHAVIORS THAT CAN KILL A RELATIONSHIP

There are many ways to degrade and finally destroy a relationship. These are four common behaviors that should be avoided:

1. Selfishness.

A focus on "me, myself and I" is not a good way to build an intimate and happy relationship. Once I (Marie) spoke to a lady who was desperately looking for companionship, and I asked her what is most important to her in a relationship. Her reply was: *"I want the guy to have at least a Master's degree. I want him to drive his own car because I don't want to drive him around. And lastly, I want him to love me more than I love him."* She was serious, and I was thinking that there may be a reason or two why she still haven't found a partner...

Selfishness is a sure way to kill any relationship, as it doesn't consider other people, and in this case your partner.

"Intensely selfish people are always very decided as to what they wish. They do not waste their energies in considering the good of others." - Marie Louise de la Ramée

2. Criticism.

To criticize is to express someone's faults in a disapproving way or express a judgment on someone. Avoid criticizing your partner by giving negative remarks such as *"You always talk about yourself,"* or sarcastic remarks such as *"You are never wrong, Mr. Perfect!"* Other examples could be saying things like, *"YOU are tired? How about me? I've been with the kids the whole day and all you do when you come home is to watch TV. Come on, give me a break!"* Or how about, *"You are always so selfish! You never think about me!"*

As criticism begins to surface in the relationship, it is a sure way to start destroying intimacy. Even though you may dislike certain traits or actions of your partner, be very careful what you say. **Demeaning words in front of your partner or in front of others are more damaging than most people think**. Your words have power to build up or to destroy. Instead, find a good time to talk to your partner about things that you don't agree with (see further down in this chapter on how to talk to your partner about sensitive issues.) If criticism isn't dealt with, contempt sooner or later rears its ugly head, and then the end of that relationship may be very near.

3. Abuse.

When abuse starts to happen in the relationship, it must quickly be dealt with, before too much harm is done. **If you are in an abusive relationship, you must first and foremost ask yourself "is my life in danger?"** If you say yes, we advise you to leave the relationship immediately, and seek help. You may or may not be able to mend the relationship back again, but your partner needs help, and you need protection, so take a step back and evaluate the situation. You can consider separating for a restricted period of time while both of you are thinking through your relationship, getting professional help and/or considering if/when to move back together again. Common forms of abuse are verbal, physical, sexual and emotional abuse. If you find yourself being a victim of any of these forms of abuse, you need help. The first step should be to ensure your own safety. Secondly, make sure your partner is aware that there is an issue present that is unacceptable (for example verbal abuse, such as using demeaning words). The third step would be to seek professional help.

4. Poor communication.
A common reason for couples to break up is poor communication. In our work with individuals and couples, we have also found that this is one of the most common reasons why couples split and/or end up in divorce.

In this chapter, we are going to focus on point number 4, namely communication. Since poor communication is believed to be a main reason for divorce and breakups, **meaningful and enjoyable communication with your partner/spouse would be a prerequisite for a strong relationship or marriage**. The way you and your partner communicate with one another is vital.

WHAT IS COMMUNICATION?

Communication is absolutely necessary for any relationship to exist. Communication involves two or more persons, where one or both seek to convey information through verbal or non-verbal means. Communication includes both talking and listening, where **listening is as important as talking**. The one who speaks should seek to communicate in a way that the other person can understand, and the listener should seek to perceive the intended meaning of what is being said. On top of that, communication involves the non-verbal message a person sends, such as body language and tone of voice.

WHAT MESSAGE IS GETTING THROUGH?

It is said that when two people talk, 6 possible messages can get through:

1. What you MEAN to say.

2. What you ACTUALLY say.

3. What the other person HEARS.

4. What the other person THINKS he or she hears.

5. What the other person SAYS ABOUT what you said.

6. What you THINK the other person said about what you said.

SO MUCH MORE THAN WORDS

Professor Albert Mehrabian, is most famous for his communication studies. He came to the conclusion that there are three elements in any face-to-face communication:

- Words

- Tone of voice

- Nonverbal behavior

He found in most cases that the nonverbal behavior (body language) accounts for as much as 55% of the message a person sends, while the tone of voice accounts for 38% and words only for 7%[7] However, he also concluded that it is obvious that nonverbal behavior isn't always more important than the words someone speaks. An example could be, "I will see you on Friday at 3 p.m." The nonverbal features are predominantly important for communicating feelings and attitudes, especially when they are inconsistent. For example, if the tone of voice and the nonverbal behavior deviates from the words spoken, people tend to believe the tone of voice and the body language more than the actual words spoken. So **be alert to what message you send through your body posture, facial expressions, tone of voice, movements, eye contact etc**. It plays a so much bigger part than we think. Attitudes and emotions are being transmitted through both what you say, how you say it and how you are acting while you're saying it.

With this in mind, you can imagine that more than often, what you say can be interpreted in different ways. Have you ever argued about something and said, *"I didn't say that,"* or *"That's not what I meant?"* Does it sound familiar? Do you want to know how to make sure you don't convey the wrong message to someone? Use paraphrasing.

THE POWER OF PARAPHRASING

With the above possible messages when two people communicate, it is good and advisable to reconfirm what the other person just said by paraphrasing. You can use expressions such as: *"It sounds to me like you are worried for..."* or *"Am I correct to say that you're upset because..."* or *"...Did I get you right when you said...?"* or *"Sorry, just to clarify, are you saying that..."* **This creates clarity and understanding**. Just ensure you don't overdo it by paraphrasing every single sentence, but do it now and then to clarify what's been said.

MEANINGFUL AND ENJOYABLE COMMUNICATION BEGINS WITH RESPECT

So how can we communicate with enjoyment and fulfillment? It all starts with respect. To soar high in your love relationship, your attitude towards your partner will be the most important and determining factor for how well you can communicate. So consider whether your attitude is set right; that there are no underlying negative thoughts and emotions such as contempt in your heart. **Your emotions are your responsibility**. We have seen how disrespectful behaviors can destroy a relationship, and bringing disrespect into communication is a sure relationship killer. So how do we communicate in a respectful way to improve our relationship?

10 KEYS TO RESPECTFUL COMMUNICATION

1. Choose to see the best in your partner.
As mentioned earlier; your attitude is critical; it will set the tone of the entire conversation. Focus on what you love with your partner, because whatever you focus on will grow larger. To see the best in your partner, you need to start to think the best of your partner. **Respect starts in the mind**. Set aside small differences and petty issues and focus on the positive. As you interact with him/her, don't become a perfectionist that requires faultless performance, but rather, choose to **see your partner as he/she truly is,** with no need to highlight every "defect." Just take an honest look at yourself and you'll probably find it easier to humbly "overlook" certain small issues with your partner. Very often we forget about our own weaknesses and mistakes as we expect our partner to be perfect. So above all, love each other deeply, because love covers mistakes.

2. Be fully present.
Listen with undivided attention; don't be distracted with other things such as glancing at your phone, watching TV or letting

others constantly interrupt as your partner speaks. Instead, aim to look him/her in the eyes and affirm with nods and words such as "OK", "oh", "I see", "mmm" etc. It is rather annoying for anyone to speak to someone who is distracted by other things such as social media, or just being "absent" in his/her thinking. People can normally sense if the other person's mind is drifting away, and distracted communication is not going to add anything good to your relationship.

Seek to really understand what your partner is trying to convey. Listen "between the lines" and try to pick up emotions and feelings behind the words that are being expressed.

3. Speak with a normal tone of voice.

No one has to raise his/her voice. Neither children nor adults respond well to raised voices or shouting; rather it usually has an opposite effect; the person shouted at generally becomes defensive and may sooner or later stop responding. Try to stay in control, **take a deep breath when you feel agitation or anger whelming up from the inside**. Keep your cool; your partner will then likely be able to feel that you respect him/her, even if you don't agree with what he/she says or does. Always remember to focus on finding a solution; not winning an argument.

4. Share what you feel with sensitivity.

Never hide your thoughts or emotions, but be sensitive how you express them. You can share your feelings and give feedback in a constructive or destructive way; **the choice is yours**. A little tip, as we have mentioned earlier, is to use *"I"* more often than *"you"*. Instead of saying *"You always say that..."* you can say: *"I feel hurt when you say that..."* or if you feel some needs are not met, you can say: *" I feel neglected in the area of... how do you feel?"*, Then *you* take responsibility for your own reactions and emotions, and the chance is greater that your partner will take in the information.

To be sensitive also includes choosing the right time to talk. The best time may be when none of you are hungry or tired, and when the children are already in bed.

5. Choose your words carefully.

Words carry tremendous power. Words can actually destroy someone's self esteem or outlook on life. Any person who constantly hears that he/she aims to nothing good or that he/she is stupid, will likely start believing the words and live out of that view of himself/herself. It is the same in a love relationship or marriage, so be careful to use your tongue to edify instead of tearing down. You can choose to speak words of contempt or words of love and respect. Remember, **spoken words cannot be unsaid**; what is being said is being said. There is nothing that hurts more than mean words from someone you love or are in a close relationship with.

A couple should be one another's greatest cheerleaders! When you speak the right words in love, it can bring life and encouragement to your partner. It adds spice to the relationship. **We live in a world that is "encouragement-deprived"**; our feeling and experience tells us that people in general doesn't receive that much of positive words of encouragement and affirmation, and as such, a couple should aim to fill that need/desire in one another's lives.

6. Let your partner finish what he/she has started expressing.

It is tempting to interrupt when you feel what is being said isn't fair, is untrue or simply disagreeable. Once again; stay in control. Train your mind and tell yourself that **you can be in control of your tongue**. Respectful conversations are conversations where both parties politely wait for the other person to finish speaking without interruptions.

5. Use paraphrasing and questions.
Instead of drawing conclusions of what your partner has expressed; consider saying things like *"It sounds to me like… is that so?"* or *"How do you think it turned out this way?"* or *"Am I correct to say that…"* alternatively *"Did I understand you correctly that…"* etc. **This is a respectful way to conclude that what you heard was what your partner meant**, and can also be a doorway to further discussions on how to solve a certain issue.

7. Don't become defensive.
Don't protect yourself by being defensive and shifting the blame, e.g. *"It's not **my** fault that… it's **your** fault".* Stick to the problem; never become personal, attacking each other.

Don't get into the "blame game" when your partner shares something you disagree with. Blame often makes your partner defensive. And furthermore, he/she may attack you in response. Blame is mostly counterproductive. **Blame also brings shame**. If you start to blame, shame and shout at your partner, ask yourself what the reasons may be that you react this way? Are you having dormant anger and resentment towards your partner? Do you yourself have areas in your life that need to be dealt with, such as guilt, shame or anger? Or is the reason for your reaction due to some outward circumstances such as lack of sleep or stress? If yes, do seek help if you need to; otherwise you are like a land mine; when someone "steps on you", you "explode."

8. Refuse emotional and verbal withdrawal.
Some people deal with conflict by withdrawing emotionally and refuse to communicate at all. The reason could be many: fear of conflict, sense of not knowing what to say, difficulty to express emotions, pride or convenience. But this emotional and/or verbal shutdown won't lead to anything positive; rather, it would distance you both more. **Be mature enough to face the problem and talk**

it out. If you need a little time to cool down before communicating, that is fine, but do tell your partner about it. If you find it hard to express how you feel, aim to learn becoming better at it.

9. Seek to converse on deeper levels.
As a couple, don't *stay* on a level of clichés or "weather talk" such as *"How was your day?"* or *"What do you want for dinner?"* but **seek to go deeper in your conversations by sharing own ideas and emotions, fears and dreams, motives and desires**, in an honest but yet respectful manner. You will find that this will deepen your love and sense of unity with one another, as you start to gain more understanding of each other. Especially men usually need to work more on communicating emotions since they, in general, are not so emotionally expressive.

HOW TO COMMUNICATE WITH YOUR PARTNER ABOUT SENSITIVE ISSUES

Sometimes sensitive issues need to be discussed. It can be topics such as money, sex, in-laws or bad habits. It is important to learn to approach these topics wisely, so here are some helpful principles that can make the conversation more effective.

- Take proper time to prepare what to say and how to say it. Anticipate questions or concerns that your partner may have and how to answer them wisely.

- Let your partner know beforehand that you would like to talk about a certain topic so that he/she is also prepared for it.

- Put yourself in your partner's shoes. How would your partner feel when you share what is in your heart?

- Choose a place free from distractions, for instance noise, mobile devices and other people.

- Select an appropriate time (such as when you both are not hungry or tired).

- Speak calmly and lovingly without confronting or lecturing.

- Take note of your body language (for example no folded arms or rolling of eyes).

- Focus on the topic and how it has impacted you (without accusing the other person).

- Share your desired outcome.

- Listen to your partner without interrupting.

- Discuss possible solutions.

- Set a time to discuss this topic again in order to evaluate your progress.

FIND MUTUAL UNDERSTANDING

It is believed that an average man speaks about 15000 words a day while a woman speaks about 30000 words a day. If this is true, we can understand that this may be an issue in many relationships. If let's say the husband comes home after a day at work and has used up his 15000 words, he doesn't really feel like talking to his wife. But she on the other hand, has been home with the kids and only used up 10000 words. Hence, she has 20000 more to go and has a need to speak to a lot her husband. Here, **mutual understanding is crucial**.

The husband may need to put in effort to listen to his wife and talk with her, even when he doesn't feel like it, just like the wife should be sensitive to her husband, and recognize when he doesn't feel like talking that much. The bottom line is meeting the needs of the other person and aim for mutual understanding. Be sensitive and "give in" to your partner now and then if he/she has a need to talk. Likewise, if your partner needs some space and don't feel like talking, give him/her that space.

Learning to have respectful conversations with your partner is an essential key to a strong love relationship. If you treat your partner with respect, the chance is high that he/she will do the same for you, and you can build a mutually enjoyable and lasting relationship.

RELATIONSHIP BUILDERS:

1. Take some time to reflect if any of the four ways to kill a relationship have crept into *your* relationship. If yes, make a decision to remove that dangerous attitude or behavior from your life. Seek professional help if needed.

2. Go through the ten keys to respectful communication and see which one you need to improve the most. Work on that key for this week as you communicate with your partner.

3. Practice paraphrasing during your next conversation, but let it be genuine and only when necessary.

4. Make a decision to avoid using *"always"* and *"never"* in the "wrong" context for one month. You will likely discover that you have minimized arguments.

POINTS TO PONDER

- Selfishness is a sure relationship killer. Give unconditionally of yourself.
- Esteem your partner higher than yourself.
- Demeaning words about your partner in front of him/her are more damaging than you can imagine.
- Your words have the power to build up and the power to destroy. Decide to be a builder of your relationship.
- Communication is the process of sharing something with another person in such a way that the other person understands what you are saying.
- We don't only speak with words; we communicate with our tone of voice and body language.
- Your attitude in your communication determines your altitude in the same.
- Winning an argument makes you a loser; creating a solution makes you a winner.
- Be fully present when you interact with your partner.
- Above all, love each other deeply, because love covers mistakes.

CHAPTER 4

RELIANCE

Build the Right Environment for Love to come Ablaze

In our aim to **get the love in our relationship ablaze**, we have so far talked about the importance of making a decision. We have also discussed how to minimize and deal with conflicts in a relationship by showing respect for each other. We then moved on to understand how we communicate effectively and how we understand each other better. Our next topic is reliance. **In order to go deeper in any relationship, developing reliance is absolutely necessary.**

THE BEDROCK OF EVERY RELATIONSHIP

Every relationship in life must have one foundational building block, and that is reliance, which is a *trust* in one's partner. A relationship cannot last or even go deeper unless there is mutual reliance. Integrity and trust must be prized above the relationship itself. **Trust is the bedrock that makes any relationship work.** It is the basis for love and intimacy. If you don't feel there is any trust in your relationship, probably you shouldn't be together at all; unless you already promised one another love for life through marriage. Then it is strongly advisable to work hard on building the trust back (we will cover that later in this chapter).

When there is no more trust, the relationship easily becomes bitter with feelings of fear and insecurity. A sense of suspicion can cause arguments and never-ending questions like: *"Why are you so late after work?" "Where have you been?"* and *"Who did you talk to?"* This kind of questioning can become the substance of daily conversations. Therefore, **building reliance is of crucial value for a healthy and thriving relationship**. Dr. Robb Thompson says, *"The mark of a healthy relationship is security, which is a result of trust."*[8] Trust makes your relationship happy and fulfilling!

RELIANCE IS CRUCIAL IN EVERY ASPECT OF A RELATIONSHIP

As you live your life and grow in your relationship, trust constantly needs to be built. As a happy relationship rests on a foundation of trust, it is wise to put in effort to create it. Trust and reliance is needed in every aspect of a relationship. The aspect that many people would likely think about first when they hear about trust and reliance is sexual intimacy.

As sexual intimacy is the closest you can get and the most precious gift you can share with another person, **sexual fidelity is critical to a healthy and happy relationship**. Keeping your commitment to be sexually faithful to your partner is crucial for trust to be present. It is definitely possible to recover from an affair (sexual unfaithfulness), which we will talk more about in chapter 5. We are aware of all the different sexual views that might be practiced, but sharing a partner or buying sexual favors outside a relationship will never bring it deeper and it will in no way deepen the love for "the one." It's mostly just an expression of lust.

Trust also needs to be built in the area of a general commitment to each other. Anger, conflict and disagreements are unavoidable. Allow one another to disagree and be angry, but build trust in such a way that you both feel secure that neither of you will abandon the other when that happens. How do you do that? **Never ever use the threat of leaving, or if married, divorcing your partner**. Don't even think about or use what we call the "D-word" (Divorce), because once you start to use it, you will surely be tempted to use it again and again until it may become a fact. If you already started, make a decision to stop using it. Remember that there is power in your words. Very often you confess something into reality. So start speaking positively about your relationship. Build it up instead of tearing it down. If you really feel that your relationship is crashing, start to say things like, *"We will work this out"* and *"It will be better after this than it was previously."* We think you get the point. It's much like a lie that is being told enough times to make a person believe it is the truth.

When you love your partner for the simple fact that he/she is the unique, precious and special person that he/she is, it creates trust. There should be no hidden motives such as looks and money. We once met a lady in a coaching session that expressed that she married her husband so she could stay permanently in the country where he was a citizen. Another lady told us that she married her husband because he was very affluent. These are very sad life stories. **Live with a pure conscience** by having clear motives *why* you are together as a couple. Love your partner in a way that makes him/her feel special and precious for who he/she is.

TRUST THRIVES IN AN ATMOSPHERE OF SAFETY AND SECURITY

When both partners feel safe and secure with each other, trust becomes an instinctive outcome. To hurt one another physically, sexually or verbally or reject one another only leads to distress and anxiety that will destroy the respect and trust in the other person. Control is another way of quickly destroying a relationship. Using blackmail or threats, or becoming possessively dependent on your partner, crying to get one's way, or exaggerate sickness to get attention, will eventually drive your partner away. Therefore, avoid behaviors such as these described.

DON'T TAKE EACH OTHER FOR GRANTED

If you are married, on your wedding day, you promised to love, honor and cherish each other for life. It is important not to take one another for granted. You shouldn't be careless or neglecting in your relationship, nor give too much time and energy to other things and people in your life, because if you do, you will surely break that trust. Build trust by making your relationship a top priority.

It's like building a skyscraper – if you don't spend enough time and build a solid foundation, you cannot build high enough. Trust is like the foundation, which the remainder of the relationship rests upon. If you don't build trust, you will limit how far your relationship can go. **Make your partner and your marriage a top priority in life**, and remember; every plant needs water to grow. If you leave it uncared for, it will wither away. **A relationship is very much like a plant. The more you care for it, the more it will grow**.

TRUST STARTS IN YOUR MIND

Remember, reliance and trust **starts in your mind**; in the thoughts you think about your partner. The same goes for mistrust. A desire of having an affair always starts in the mind, and therefore, it is very important to protect your thought life. **You can choose what thoughts you allow to be entertained in your mind**. You can't help a fleeting thought to come, but you can choose to entertain it or reject it. Think and believe the best about your partner; that he/she has the best of intentions and can make wise decisions as well as be trusted with anything and everything. We don't talk about you being naïve and denying facts if there are obvious areas of mistrust. However, the point is to focus on the positive in your partner.

For trust to be built, **trust must be the basic *belief* in the other person**, and as the relationship goes from shallow to deep, it must be continuously showed. If both parties choose to believe in the best intention of the other, both persons will also perform better. When you trust your partner, there is no reason to hide things from one another. When you believe in each other, honesty and openness can be present. An "open book policy" will not be something complicated, but it'll be natural to share things with each other.

THE OPEN BOOK POLICY

Honesty and openness is a must. There is no reason to hide things from one another. If you are afraid to let your partner see some of your "private" things, you may not be transparent enough or maybe you have something to hide? Avoid creating unnecessary suspicion in your partner. There is no way you can build deep love and at the same time hide things or lying to each other. A couple shouldn't control each other, but openness builds trust and intimacy in the relationship.

If your partner wants to know, be open about your whereabouts, who you meet etc., not because you don't trust one another but because you do. There is no reason not to tell. To know one another's whereabouts **creates security and oneness in your relationship.** Our suggestion is an "open book policy" for your relationship, where nothing is secret, but there is total openness and honesty. A couple that applies the open book policy opens up and shares things on purpose as they know that it will build trust and greater intimacy. This has nothing to do with trying to control, but to create trust, security and intimacy. **Secrecy is a killer for any relationship, as it will destroy intimacy**. Make a decision from an early stage of your relationship to be a team where there is openness, honesty and trust.

THE POWER OF TRANSPARENCY

The more you get to know one another, the more you can feel secure to open up and share your hearts. This takes time. Remember, as trust deepens, vulnerability is no longer a weakness but strength. **You are so totally safe in the relationship that you can be 100% open and honest**. That can deepen the relationship more. As you get to know each other more and more through the years, sharing everything from dreams and fears to good and bad childhood memories, you will likely find that the love for one another increases. Why is that so? Because the more you know about a person, the background where he/she came from, the life he/she have lived and the experiences he/she have had, the more you will understand his/her needs and be eager to lovingly meet those needs, and so the love deepens.

Furthermore, in a relationship of trust, you will not be afraid of showing your flaws, from your unruly hair on Sunday morning to your fear of darkness, phobias or whatever it may be. In a relationship of trust, you create an environment of love where there is freedom to share about your weaknesses. **Reliance and trust is being built where there is transparency**, and where there is transparency or "light," there can be no closet ghosts or dark secrets.

CHARACTER'S CORNERSTONE

One element of trust is faithfulness. **Faithfulness is the cornerstone of character**. Henry Ford gave a reply on his 50th wedding anniversary when asked about his marital bliss and how longevity was possible. He replied, "Just the same as in the automobile business, stick to one model."[9] This is a great example of faithfulness. How can a couple not only stay together, but still remain in love with one another after years and even decades? They have placed **a high value on faithfulness**; they once promised to love each other for life, and they would stay faithful to that promise, no matter what.

TRUST IN RELATION TO FORGIVENESS

Laura Luchies, Assistant Director of the Calvin College Center for Social Research, says that **trust appears to distort people's memory of the past**.[10] As such, when the foundation of trust is there, the chances that mistakes will be seen as onetime events, are greater. When a person trusts his/her partner, even when one's partner does make blunders and mistakes, there is a greater grace towards the other person. **A trusting person becomes more gracious and forgiving towards others!** The opposite is also true. When there is no trust, you will see through the lens of mistrust, and even a small issue becomes big and serious because mistrust already exists, and that makes it harder to forgive.

HAVING A "WE-MENTALITY"

In order to build a strong loving relationship of trust, having a "we-mentality" is critical. We can't help but wonder occasionally about couples we meet, why they are in a relationship at all. They are so selfish and full of their own things, planning everything around themselves and what they want, going out alone with their friends, playing golf when they want, buying what they want without ever considering their partner. Furthermore, they make sure that there is always an escape clause in the relationship. **It's like living a single life but yet under the same roof with someone else**. Why get into a relationship in the first place then? Sometimes it's fascinating how so many people who are in a relationship want to get out of it and at the same time, so many that are single want to get in to one.

A relying couple (particularly if they are married) tells one another *"Everything I am and have is yours."* There is **a commitment to live and function as a team** and commit every inch of life and self to one another. There is a "we-mentality." You are still two individuals but yet there is a great sense of unity and team spirit. When you become "one" in every aspect of life such as sharing emotions and dreams, discussing your common financial goals, parenting and what to do on a weekend or holiday, your relationship will flourish and blossom. A sense of oneness and unity doesn't happen overnight, so give yourselves time to build that team spirit in your relationship. **Everything you think, say and do in relation to each other will either bring you closer or further apart**. Be a relationship builder in all you do. Avoid living like a single in a relationship by building unity through involvement.

CREATE A "WE-MENTALITY" THROUGH INVOLVEMENT

Involve each other in your daily affairs. An example: You are planning for some financial investments and you are reading reports about the current stock market as you scratch your head, considering where to invest. Your wife is sitting next to you and asks you what you are doing. Your wife is not interested in stock investments at all, but to create greater unity, you take a little time to explain your options to her; what the pros and the cons are, and even ask her what she thinks.

Or you came home from work as a doctor and you carried out a very difficult and complicated surgery, and as such, you are exhausted and don't feel like talking to anyone. Your husband comes and asks how your day was. You can choose to be short and say "OK" or you can involve your husband, even though he knows nothing about carotid endarterectomy in the arteries. You explain lovingly how it works and what happened during the surgery. Once again, ***involving*** one another creates a "we-mentality."

THE DAMAGE OF LOST TRUST

We have found that the loss of trust is a major problem in many relationships. Whether there has been lying, sexual unfaithfulness, gambling away money or other reasons for the loss of trust, great damage is done to the person that was cheated. The behaviors that caused the loss of trust are usually hard to change, because they are usually complex and have often been going on for a long period of time before a couple comes to the stage where they desperately want a change. The problem is that **once mistrust and suspicion set in, it will keep escalating unless it is dealt with**. When a person is observed through the lens of suspicion and mistrust, it has the potential to affect the perception of everything that person says or does. That is why it is of vital importance to deal with every negative thought, because a thought soon becomes words and finally the words becomes actions...

"Sow a thought and you reap an action; sow an action and you reap a habit; sow a habit and you reap a character; sow a character and you reap a destiny." - Ralph Waldo Emerson

COMMON REASONS FOR LOST TRUST

There are plenty of reasons why a person fails to trust his/her partner or a couple struggle to trust each other. Some common reasons are:

Lack of Openness and Honesty: When a person refuses to open up about his/her personal life such as talking about work, plans, dreams and emotions, trust can easily vanish. Do aim for an "open book policy" as mentioned earlier in this chapter. Remember that you are better off if you function as a team. When you have built a habit of openness, it is much easier to discuss problems in a constructive way and you will feel closer to one another. This is more often a problem for men and much more so if the man is introvert in his personality. But that cannot be an excuse; rather, openness can be learned and practiced.

Failure to keep Promises and Commitments: A habit of not sticking to what has been promised causes a sense of lost trust. When promises have been broken again and again, it often happens that what is being said is received with a "pinch of salt;" "well, he didn't do what he said the past few times, why would he do it now?" **Decide to be a promise keeper.** If you are unsure about whether you would be able to keep a promise, don't say anything. **Let your yes be a yes and no be a no**. Keeping promises builds security and trust in any relationship. Practice to say what you mean and mean what you say.

Sexual Unfaithfulness: To be sexually unfaithful is probably the most serious form of betrayal (read more in chapter 5 on how to deal with this kind of difficult and complex situation.) Even though we live in a world where many couples have experienced this and some even think it is OK, we have a firm belief that sexual unfaithfulness always will be damaging to a relationship.

Platonic or Emotional attachments to another person: To develop a close attachment with the opposite sex outside of one's relationship can be as serious as sexual unfaithfulness. This is where a person confides in the other person and opens up about personal problems and relationship issues, and creates a dependent and affectionate relationship outside of his/her own relationship. This is dangerous as it often leads to sexual unfaithfulness. It is crucial to set boundaries when spending time alone with people of the opposite gender. It could be boundaries such as never spending time alone with the opposite sex, deciding not to share personal things that you wouldn't want your partner to hear you are sharing, and to be accountable to your partner where you are at all times. "It is easier to avoid temptation than to resist it." In other words, don't put yourself in a situation where you can be tempted to do something you regret later. A moment of pleasure isn't worth the long-term pain and the consequences attached to it. And bear in mind that sexual contact according to the United States legal system is only at the level of *"having an intention to touch, directly or through the clothing, of the genitalia, anus, groin, breast, inner thigh, or buttocks with an intent to arouse or gratify the sexual desire of any person."*[11]

Pornography: Pornography is very destructive for any relationship. It can have a seemingly harmless beginning such as reading magazines with sexual content or watching images online, but those images usually "get stuck" in the brain, causing sexual fantasies which often leads to a desire for more, and starts a downward spiral. You can read more about the negative effects of pornography and how to break free from it in chapter 5.

In short, these are 5 common reasons for lost trust: a lack of openness and honesty, failure to keep promises and commitments, sexual unfaithfulness, platonic or emotional attachment to another person and pornography. These are "traps" to look out for in your relationship. If you find yourself or your partner stuck in any of these behaviors, don't fret. There is a way out. So where do you start if your relationship is on the rocks and you both desire to work it out? Below are six practical steps for how to rebuild trust.

SIX PRACTICAL STEPS FOR HOW TO REBUILD TRUST

If you and your partner have an issue of distrust, but both have a willing attitude to work things out, we would advise you to take the following practical steps:

1. Face the Problem

You need to fully face the problem at hand in order for trust to be rebuilt and the process of restoration to even start. This is the very first step that must be taken. If a person *can't see* there is a problem or he/she doesn't *want to see*, then nothing can be done to change. **Let down your guards and stop denying or delaying**

dealing with the issues. Humility is needed here. You've got to throw away all pride and fear of "losing face;" let your partner see and hear "your naked you." This includes facing all facets of the problem, including your own contribution to it. As you begin to honestly face the problem and come to terms with how it really is, you will be ready for the next step.

2. Talk it Out

Give one another time and space to vent feelings. Don't defend yourself or be too causal about what has happened; it will never work. Just "throw the cards on the table"; open up and share about the struggles you face. Share your concerns. **Greater understanding often leads to greater intimacy**. Remember to not interrupt, but instead let your partner finish what he/she would like to say. Even though you may not agree on certain things or feel some information is untrue or unfair, just keep your mouth sealed until it is your turn. As you communicate, listen with your whole being and speak with respect. Watch out for the "blame game" with comments such as "But you said...", "But that was because you..." and "I wouldn't have said that if you didn't..." **Blame shifting will never lead anywhere, but will rather escalate the intensity of the conversation**. (You can read more about communication in chapter 3.)

3. Ask for Forgiveness

Do take *full* responsibility for what you yourself have done. Leave it to your partner to settle from his/her side. Ask *genuinely* for forgiveness and don't expect an immediate "yes, sure!" If you have hurt your partner, **it may take a little time for him/her to forgive**, but that is really up to your partner. If you have asked for forgiveness, you have done your first part.

Restitution is the next part of your responsibility. It means to compensate or make it up to the other person. If you were unfaithful, you cannot rewind time and pretend it didn't happen, but you can do your best to make it up to your partner. **In dialogue with him/her, find out in what ways you can make it up**. It could be through being very open and accountable of your whereabouts and who you are with, or it could be to come home directly after work most of the weeknights (see more under point 5 below.) Many couples testify that after a "big storm" when the calmness of forgiveness and reconciliation sets in, the relationship actually flourishes and deepens even more.

4. Practice the Four A:s

After you both have reconciled (or even in the time lapse while you are waiting for your partner to release forgiveness to you), we advise you to apply these 4 steps to demonstrate your love for your partner:

Affection

When you demonstrate affection, you show your love physically. Affection can be expressed through touch, such as stroking your partner's hair, putting your arm around him/her or holding his/her hand. It could also be through hugging and kissing.

Appreciation

When you appreciate a person, you value that person and gratefully acknowledge the qualities and uniqueness about him/her. Do develop a grateful heart and be an appreciative person towards your partner.

Attention

When you give attention to your partner, you show respect by taking notice of him/her and what he/she says. Take note of all the little things and be encouraging. For example *"You look really great in that dress"*, *"I notice you washed the car, thanks,"* or *"Thank you so much for cooking such a delicious dinner."* As we mentioned earlier, don't take each other and one another's efforts for granted.

Assurance

Express that you believe in your relationship by reassuring your love regularly to your partner.

In summary, practicing the 4 A:s is to, on a regular basis, hug and kiss your partner, treat him/her as unique, special and important; don't take him/her for granted, and choose to fully trust.

5. Make a Plan for Change

As you rebuild trust, especially if you are the one that let down your partner, you will need to put in extra effort to show him/her that you can be trusted again.

Things you can do could be to:

- **Cut off ALL contact with any third party**. If there was a betrayal of platonic or sexual nature, this is critical.

- **Keep your promises at all cost**. Even small things such as calling when you say you will call are important. Let there be no lies and no excuses.

- **Be "overly accountable"**. Be transparent about where you are going, with whom you are meeting etc. This may be a hard practice, but it is part of the cost of rebuilding trust and reliance.

- **Be prepared for setbacks**. The way back may be a bumpy road that sometimes feels like you are taking one step forward and two steps back.

- **Meet your partner's needs according to the 4 A:s above**. Find out what your partner desires. Do your best to meet those needs joyfully and quickly.

- **Confide in someone**. Have a venue to "pour out your heart." Most of us would need someone to share with when things get tough. Within the frame of confidentiality, to protect your partner, find someone that you feel easy sharing with. It can be a close friend or talking to God. It can be just being alone and writing down your thoughts and feelings on a piece of paper.

Be careful about sharing sensitive issues involving your partner with your family members. They will most likely take your side, wanting to protect you, and may not give constructive feedback. It may affect how they perceive your partner in the future. **Children should at all cost stay out of any conflict between mum and dad**. You would want to protect your partner from negative thoughts from others, especially your own children.

6. Dream Together

In order for you to build your relationship to last for a long time, you would need to have common dreams/goals. Maybe you had a dream when you first started out, but it has been shattered by life's problems and circumstances.

Start by talking to each other about what is in your heart and what you desire to see in the future. You can discuss aspects such as marriage, baby planning, trips, what kind of home you would like to have, financial plans, common interests, values, and more (read more about common goals and values in chapter 8.)

There is a need to discuss values about living life together. This may be one of the most important part of the entire reconciliation process, so do spend time talking about what you desire and how you both can move forward together.

You will find that **sharing common dreams and goals draws you closer to each other.** As you embark on the road of rebuilding the trust so that you can rely totally on one another (again), you will likely find that your relationship starts to bring lots of happiness and fulfillment.

HOPE FOR THE HOPELESS

Author Shannon L. Alder once said: *"Your dignity can be mocked, abused, compromised, toyed with, lowered and even badmouthed, but it can never be taken from you. You have the power today to reset your boundaries, restore your image, start fresh with renewed values and rebuild what has happened to you in the past."* [12]

Whatever the problem is, **there is hope for any broken down relationship**. If both parties are willing to get to work and give it some time, the odds are great that things not only will work out in the relationship, but the relationship will be stronger and happier than before. As long as you don't make the decision *not to* give the affection anymore to your partner, you have good odds to build up your relationship again. And as you emerge strongly from a broken down relationship, it can even be set as an example for others to see, that there is hope for even the seemingly most hopeless couple situation.

SECURITY

For a relationship to be healthy and harmonious, both parties must feel totally secure in it, and in order for it to be secure, there must be mutual trust present. What would be better than to feel fully secure in the arms of your partner? A place where there is no doubt, but only safety and protection? Whether you start to rebuild or you long to deepen the trust and reliance with your partner, it may be a long and bumpy road, but it will all be worth it.

RELATIONSHIP BUILDERS

1. Go through the "Five crucial areas of reliance" found in the beginning of this chapter, and ask your partner to do the same. Then share your results with one another.

    If your partner is not willing, you can do it yourself. It may give you some new insights about your relationship and/or you might learn things about yourself.

2. Select one area that you will start to work on (e.g. the open book policy or one of the 4 A:s; wherever you feel you want to see an improvement). Commit to actively demonstrating it to your partner during the next three weeks. Why three weeks? Because **it takes at least three weeks to create a new habit**.

3. Write down what you've done as well as the results you see after three weeks. Evaluate your progress.

POINTS TO PONDER

- Trust is the bedrock that makes any relationship work.
- Words you speak can change the world around you. If you are not happy with what you experience, begin by speaking differently and you'll see what happens.
- When you believe in the best intentions of your partner, both will "perform" better.
- Faithfulness is the cornerstone of character.
- Character is the foundation of trust and security in any relationship.
- If you are in a relationship, don't live like you're single.
- Relationship is a lot about "we-mentality." Start to think more in terms of "WE" and you will have a different outcome.
- Protect your own relationship by respecting the personal space and unspoken boundaries when interacting with someone else of the opposite gender.
- You're a team; work together to achieve your dream.
- Involving one another creates a sense of unity.
- Your word is your bond; keep your promises to your partner. Let your yes be yes and no be no.
- In sexual intimacy: be respectful and loving, never force your partner to do anything he/she is not comfortable with.
- Give of yourself and don't only have sex when YOU feel like it.
- Sexual intimacy in marriage builds stronger bonds between you both.

CHAPTER 5

REBOUND

How to Bounce Back after a Relationship Setback

Every couple struggles in their relationship from time to time. There may be various challenges, damages and setbacks. There could be plenty of reasons for that, but there are in particular two issues that seem to cause more severe damage to a relationship than others. Perhaps these two are also the toughest to bounce back from.

When a couple is having serious problems, the road back to intimacy can be long and bumpy. However, it is surely possible to rebound. To rebound can be defined in several ways; "To increase or improve after a recent decrease or decline"[13] and "To bounce back after hitting a hard surface."[14] **Love and intimacy can surely rebound after a setback**. Some couples even testify that their relationship grew deeper after storms hit and they bounced back together.

STATISTICS SPEAKS FOR ITSELF

One large-scale survey including over 100,000 people revealed that 33% of the men and 19% of the women admitted that they had been sexually unfaithful[15]. On top of this, there are likely an additional number of unknown cases. We can easily conclude that infidelity is one of the major issues for many couples.

Dr. Patrick F. Fagan writes in his research thesis that the use of pornography is a pathway to infidelity and divorce, and is many times considered a major cause in these crises in families[16]. It was concluded that both spouses perceive **pornography viewing as**

equivalent to infidelity. Furthermore, Dr. Fagan also mentioned that it was discovered that the use of pornography increases the rate of sexual unfaithfulness with 300%.

As a result of these findings including many others, and in combination with hearing couples share their struggles; we conclude that infidelity and pornography are two very common issues couples face. Furthermore, many times one or both parties feel hopeless and without a clue what to do, so here we will share with you some advise on what to do if you feel you are in a helpless situation due to infidelity or pornography.

INFIDELITY

Infidelity is to be unfaithful to one's spouse or sexual partner. Some call it EMA (extramarital affair) if the couple is married, and others talk about cheating. Basically it is the same thing – to be disloyal towards one's partner. Infidelity is often associated with secrecy and lies, and brings a distance in the relationship. Hence, when there is infidelity present in a relationship, the couple often breaks up when the cheated partner finds out. Often, infidelity leads to divorce. However, as mentioned earlier, many couples do rebound and emerge stronger.

What are some reasons that people are unfaithful then? They are many, but infidelity often happens in work related situations such as business trips, office parties and other company events. Many times with alcohol in the picture, and the partner not around, the temptation escalates and translates into actions. Other common reasons are unhappiness with one's own sex-life, unmet emotional needs in the relationship, and boredom. Some curiously seek for an adventure and see the fling as something that can bring them excitement and emotional recognition. Others have a high sex-drive or even seek revenge from being betrayed themselves.

Generally, gratification of one's self in various forms often is the main reason why someone is unfaithful to his/her partner.

Whatever the reason for the infidelity in a relationship is, the betrayed partner will often feel very hurt and abandoned. So if you are the person that has been/are sexual unfaithful towards your partner, you've got some things to work on. What do you do if you are the one that made the mistake and committed infidelity? It may not have been intentional, but a wrong decision was made in a moment when your guard was down. Here are some critical things to do if you have in mind to save your relationship:

BREAKING FREE FROM INFIDELITY

Cut off the relationship with the person you had an affair with. Stop seeing the person you've been unfaithful with. Erase phone numbers, email addresses, Facebook accounts etc. and make a firm decision that you won't have anything to do with that person again. Let your partner know by your actions that you are serious. **Words alone won't do**. It is critical that you do this and let your partner know when it is done. If the person contacts you or you bump into each other in a public place, let your partner know. If you work at the same place, let your contact be purely professional and stop interacting with the person when no one else is around. If you work very closely and there are no other people around, consider changing jobs. What is more important to you – your spouse/partner/family or your job?

Ask for forgiveness. To take a step to genuinely ask for forgiveness is vital for you to show your partner that you're serious about your relationship. **Ask without expecting an immediate release from your partner**. Instead, be prepared for anger and tears. The betrayal you have caused is huge and it may take time for your partner, if he/she comes to that stage, to forgive. Be patient and give your partner space to vent his/her anger and grief.

Provide details about the affair if requested by your partner. Secrecy doesn't belong in a love relationship. Put the facts on the table and start to build a culture of openness in between you both. Reveal as much as your partner asks for. It may help him/her walk trough the emotional trauma that has occurred. Share how it happened and why it happened, if your partner requests it.

Show extravagant empathy. The path to recovery may be long and painful. If the partner that had an affair shows extravagant empathy with his/her partner when he/she is angry or grieved, the chances of healing are greater. Keep listening to your hurt partner, even when things are repeated, and be gracious and patient. After all, that's the least you can do after the hurt you've caused your loved one.

Make restitution. Ask your partner how you can make it up to him/her. It can include things such as being seemingly "overly accountable" about your whereabouts, whom you are with etc. Take full responsibility for what you have done. **Blaming your partner will never work out**. If things haven't been well in your relationship, such as needs not being met, you can discuss that in a later stage. This is the time to focus on rebuilding trust and to show extravagant grace and empathy with your hurt partner.

Reconfirm your commitment again and again. Ask for forgiveness again if needed, and promise to never have an affair again. Your partner may have fears that it may happen again, so you need to reassure him/her that you are committed to him/her for the rest of your life.

Stay in control of your thought life. Unfaithfulness starts in the mind. Thoughts sooner or later become actions. Science today proves that your actions start with a thought.

So how do you avoid unfaithfulness? **One of the keys to avoid unfaithfulness is to think about the right things**. If you are constantly thinking about your partner's failures or his/her weaknesses, you are not enhancing the feeling of love for your partner. Think about all his/her positive traits and all the experiences you've had together.

You also need to know that **an act of unfaithfulness can start through your eyes**. The great and well-known Jesus said that if you are only looking lustfully at another man's woman, you have committed adultery.

The hormone of sexual desire is testosterone, which is the hormone of libido. Science explains that there is a connection between what you see and the sexual arousal set in your brain. **Men in particular are often profoundly affected and aroused by erotic images**. If you really think about it, why are prostitutes dressed the way they are? If they didn't know that men were so affected by it, do you think they would dress the way they do? It has been said that prostitutes from ancient civilizations would draw pictures on the outside walls of their homes, depicting naked people who were having sexual intercourse with the purpose of arousing the men who passed by. It was like an advertisement to attract men and get them hooked to buy their services.

So knowing this, **you need to set boundaries for your eyes and your mind**. What you allow yourself to see, ponder and meditate on will significantly affect you. Especially if you walk around looking at others of the opposite gender, commenting on how they look, comparing them to your partner, and having lustful thoughts about them, it will definitely not help you in rebuilding faithfulness to your partner. You have hurt your partner deeply, so now is the time to show that you are serious about repairing your relationship. You need to be strict. If you want to stay faithful, you need to control your eyes and your thoughts. To gain victory in this battle and not fall again, **determination and a strong will to renew your mind in this area is critical**.

"Human beings, by changing the inner attitudes of their minds, can change the outer aspects of their lives." – William James

As you embark on the road to reconciliation, you need to be determined and patient as it may take some time. As you are in the process, don't be too hard on yourself. Regret and releasing forgiveness is crucial, but there is also a time to let go of the past and move on towards the future. Everyone makes mistakes; so don't cling on to your mistakes forever.

RECOVERING FROM BEING A VICTIM OF INFIDELITY

Now, if you are the one that has been a victim of infidelity, can you bounce back from the fact that your partner had an affair? The answer is yes, but it may not be easy. **For a couple to find restoration, both need to have a willingness to repair the damage, build up trust again and reconnect back to intimacy**. When trust has been broken in a relationship and you have been abandoned in such a way by the one you were supposed to trust most of all, it often takes time to heal and build up that trust again. Here is some advice for you:

Express your feelings. Anger, shock, grief, sadness and frustration are common feelings that follow the knowing that your spouse/partner have been unfaithful. Be open to talk about how the affair has affected you – your disappointments, doubts and feelings of betrayal. Let your feelings be expressed, but choose *who* you share with and *how* you share it. Remember to protect your partner, despite what he/she has done. After things have settled, you wouldn't want the whole world to know about the affair, so be wise and share with someone that can keep what you share confidential. Of course you should also share with your partner how you feel. Putting words on your feelings can help in the recovery process.

Ask questions to your spouse if you feel you need to know. Sometimes it helps to know more how your spouse was thinking and what actually happened. It can help in the process of healing. Some want to know every little detail; others don't want to know anything as they feel it will cause them more hurt. Do what feels best for you.

Allow yourself time to grieve. Grief often takes time. You don't need to hurry the process and quickly get over it; rather, **let healing take its time**.

Reflect on what has happened. Take time to think through the incident. Reflect on where things went wrong. Do you have a part to play? Although infidelity is never justifiable, think through if there were something in your relationship that you did to contribute to the unfortunate event of the affair. Have needs been unmet in the relationship? Has there been a lack of love and affection? Have there been constant nagging and quarreling present? Very often there are underlying reasons why things happen. **It may not be an excuse for what has happened, but an explanation**. Recognizing that infidelity commonly is a symptom of an unhappy marriage/relationship can lead a couple to patch things up and grow closer.

Forgive. This may take time, and that is OK. With time, the painful memories can fade away. It is extremely crucial to forgive in order for you to move on in your relationship. **You can't stay in the past if you want to move on to the future.** The sooner the better, but the most important thing is to forgive from your heart, with genuine honesty. Forgiveness is more than a feeling – it is a decision you make, and thereafter the feelings would usually follow suit, so you need to be willing in your heart to forgive your partner. Just remember, **forgiveness is not approving, accepting or making wrong right; it simply releases you from the bondage of what the other person did to you.**

Open up for intimacy. When your partner has ended all contact and involvement with the former lover, help your partner to pursue you again by being open to intimacy. Don't hold back but let go of the past and try to enjoy the closeness again. Take it slowly. Bit by bit you can come back.

Seek support. If you need, you can consider seeking support from a counselor or therapist, or attending a support group for people that have been through the same issue. This usually lasts for a shorter period of time, perhaps for a few sessions, but it can be very effective.

Reconnect back with your partner. Reconnect back by spending time doing fun and romantic things without talking about the affair. Enjoy each other's company afresh. It may take tears, struggle and a lot of pain to come back once you have been betrayed or hurt in this manner. Give yourself time and do not commit abuse on yourself by brushing it off easily. Allow yourself time to heal the hurt in your life. At the same time, don't lock yourself away from your partner. **Your ultimate goal is to come back to rebuild the damage**.

CONSIDER GIVING A SECOND CHANCE

When a relationship has suffered shipwreck, the easiest thing to do is to run, in other words to leave permanently. This is true especially if you are the victim of infidelity. We would recommend you to take some time off for yourself and grieve, if and when necessary. The reason being so you can eventually make a good decision on how to move on, in your right mind; not out of anger, grief, pain or hatred. **Likely you just don't want to throw away a relationship you might have built over many years.** Of course it's extremely painful, but you may need to consider a few things: Was the affair a onetime incident? Does your partner show honest and genuine regret? Is your partner truly sorry for what he/she has done? Depending on what the answers are to these questions, you can make a wise decision what to do next. Remember that everybody can make mistakes, so don't let an incident like this erase what you have built. Consider giving your partner a second chance. **What couples have overcome together will usually make their relationship stronger and deeper**.

An old couple was asked how they managed to stay together for 65 years. The wife replied: *"We were born in a time where if something was broke, you fixed it, you didn't just throw it away..."*

PORNOGRAPHY

We believe that most people think that sexual unfaithfulness is unhealthy for a relationship, but how about pornography? What's the big deal about that?

Psychologist Patrick F. Fagan claims, "Pornography hurts adults, children, couples, families and society. Among adolescents, pornography hinders the development of a healthy sexuality, and among adults, it distorts sexual attitudes and social realities. In families, the use of pornography leads to marital dissatisfaction, infidelity, separation and divorce." [16] Therefore, **when people claim that pornography is harmless as long as it is for private use only, we believe it is far from the truth**. Rather, it does affect every relationship the person has.

WHY IS PORNOGRAPHY SO DESTRUCTIVE?

Pornography encourages comparison. Comparison can be done in areas such as looks, the act of sexual intercourse and sexual positions. It can contribute to a decreased self-esteem as it creates a feeling of not being "qualified" by being unable to live up to the false expectations of one's partner. Someone once said that **comparison is the thief of joy**. Every person wants to be seen and treated as the unique and special person he/she is without being compared to somebody else. **Comparison surely has a negative impact on the intimacy between partners**. One must not forget that pornography is not "real." The sexual act has been filmed in parts, cut and pasted together, and therefore, it does not depict a real sexual act. Actually, studies of 500 couples from varying ages and different parts of the world have shown that penetrative sex (from penetration to ejaculation) lasts on an average of 5.4 minutes.[17] When you know this, you realize that pornography is just there to get you hooked. Don't forget it is a billion dollar industry.

Pornography is highly addictive. As a person continues to expose himself/herself to pornography, a "path" will be created in the brain. It changes the brain by corrupting the way it registers pleasure, and then it sabotages other normal drives such as motivation and learning. **An addiction involves a strong craving for something, often with a sense of being out of control**; "I must have it or I'll die." One look, and it sets the addiction in motion and eventually hijacks the brain. We've had coaching sessions where individuals shared how they started to watch pornography online, and became so addicted to it that it took more and more of their time and attention, interfering significantly with their lives. In one particular case, it influenced the husband so badly that the wife couldn't live up to his fantasies, which led him to get them fulfilled by buying sexual favors from prostitutes. You can only imagine the consequences for his wife and children when they got to know about it.

Pornography invites lying. As pornography often creates shame and guilt in the person given to it, it often leads to lying. **Small secrets often grow to big lies**. Make a choice not to have any secrets and lies in your relationship. It is always better to be honest and expose problems in order for them to be solved. **To confess weakness is strength**. It just means you are human and humble enough to acknowledge that you're not perfect.

Pornography often leads to interference in daily life. A person that finds himself/herself increasingly behind the screen watching pornography often discovers that it affects him/her significantly in many areas of his/her daily life. Common symptoms of excessive pornographic exposure according to research are among others; tiredness, social anxiety, isolation, insecurity, erectile dysfunction, and lack of interest in real sex, relational issues and poor academic performance.

Pornography is a hindrance for intimacy. If pornography enters into the relationship, a third party has now invaded it. Pornography, even though it is in the area of fantasy, is betrayal towards one's partner. Some people forces their partner to watch pornography together, followed by intercourse. This is a form of sexual abuse, and you have no obligation to watch and be forced to do things you are not comfortable with. **Do not believe anyone who claims that pornography will help you as a couple to improve your sexual relationship**. Rather, it destroys everything beautiful about sex in your relationship and that for which it was created. When pornography is present in a relationship, even if it is unknown to the other partner, it causes emotional division and the distance between the partner's increases. The consequences will most likely be that one or both parties start to have a disinterest in sexual intimacy with one another. Moreover, pornography harms the relationship as it shapes the partner's sexuality and keeps increasing the physical distance in between them.

HOW TO BREAK FREE FROM PORNOGRAPHY

If you and/or your partner are stuck in pornography, here are some things you can do to break free from it. Remember, you may not be free instantly, but it may take some time to redirect your thought patterns and work on internal issues in your life.

Admit: Any counselor or therapist knows that if there is no admittance of the problem or addiction in a person's life, it is almost impossible to have a breakthrough. **Anything kept in secret is hard to break free from**. Bring light to the problem and expose it by sharing and admitting to a counselor, therapist, or anyone else with confidentiality. It will be the initial step of finding freedom.

Find understanding: Find out what the possible reasons are. Are there insecurity issues? Are needs not met in the relationship? Was it a simple temptation that escalated? You can't blame any person or circumstance for what has happened, as there are a number of active choices you've made over a period of time. But with an understanding, it is easier to find a solution.

Analyze your thought life: Analyze your thinking and your fantasies and try to understand them. Discern what your true desires are, and then seek to meet those in healthy ways.

Create accountability: Invite someone you trust to be allowed to ask tough questions. **There is power in accountability**. Just by letting someone know and having that person ask you about it on a regular basis may be so uncomfortable for you that the addiction start to lose its grip on you. Let this person support and encourage you to make wise choices.

Avoid temptation: Do what you can to avoid temptation. If you often end up behind your computer screen in the nights after your family goes to bed, you can instead go to bed at the same time as your partner. You could install a filter to block access to websites with pornographic content. Never use your laptop or computer in a closed room. Use it in public areas, such as the living room, kitchen etc. Avoid places where there are lightly dressed women. Walk a different path home if necessary. Stop associating with those friends that pull you in, until you find victory in this area.

Create new thought patterns: By using the rubber band principle, which is about disrupting unhealthy thought patterns, you can build an off-ramp. The principle is to interrupt old patterns in the brain that were previously created. It will not work just trying not to think about that unwanted thought. The more you try, the more focus you give that thought. You have to interrupt it and replace it with another thought. Place a rubber band on your wrist. When an unwanted thought occurs, snap the rubber band on your wrist in response to that thought. This will interrupt the thought process and send a signal of pain to the brain not to stay in that pathway. Thereafter, choose to think another thought immediately such as "I really love my wife." This thought now replaces that other thought. So every time you see a beautiful woman/handsome man and it sets off your emotion and fantasies, you snap the rubber band, and instead of getting the positive chemical reaction support to that thought (created by encephalin and endorphins), it receives a signal of pain. **If you immediately snap and choose another thought over 3 weeks each time the unwanted thought occurs, your brain is reconditioned and your thought pattern can be broken.** Of course you might find other ways to deal with interrupting the thought pattern than this, but the principle is the same.

Ask for forgiveness: Let your partner know that you are seriously sorry for how this has affected him/her. Forgiveness is a crucial step towards intimacy. Read more about forgiveness in chapter 2.

Pursue intimacy: Pursue your partner again and again to create emotional, physical (and spiritual) intimacy with him/her. As pornography is about self-gratification, **unselfish acts of love can create intimacy in your relationship once again**, and this often leads to great sex. Work on finding sexual fulfillment in your relationship. **Fulfilled desires minimize temptation.**

Now, what can you do if your partner is into pornography? Perhaps you find yourself in a situation where your relationship is on the rocks due to the pornographic addiction of your partner. Don't fret; there is a way to overcome it.

"MY PARTNER IS INTO PORNOGRAPHY. WHAT SHOULD I DO?"

Pornography is a form of betrayal, just like infidelity. You may feel disappointed because your partner has this "need" of watching pornography. As you find out about it, here is some advice for you:

Allow yourself to feel the way you feel. Lots of emotions may come up to the surface if you just found out that your partner is watching pornography. You perhaps felt something was wrong but you couldn't put your finger on it. The sense of being overwhelmed by your findings can saturate your emotions – emotions of betrayal, anger, sadness and frustration. Tell yourself it is OK to feel that way.

Have a dialogue with your partner. Do share with your partner how you feel. Expressing how you feel is important, as pornography doesn't affect only him/her, but you as well. Reflect on what has happened and ask questions with an aim to gain understanding of your partner. What are the reasons that he/she is into pornography? Is there a lack of meeting needs in your relationship? Do you seldom have sexual intimacy? Is there an emotional or physical distance in between you both? Do you quarrel often? Are there other frustrations or unhappiness in your relationship? Or is your partner actually having a sex addiction? All these factors can be reasons why a person is seeking satisfaction in the area of pornography. You should never take the blame for your partner's addiction; however, it is good to reflect on what can be improved in your relationship and gain a greater understanding of possible causes.

Don't blame yourself. It is common that people feel dirty or shameful because their partner is into pornography. We would want to encourage you not to take the blame for your partner's actions. Remember that your partner can still love you, even though he is watching pornography. Many times it has nothing to do with you.

Don't let pornography come in between you. We believe most people don't want to be enslaved by pornography. Because that is what it does – enslaves you. So show your partner you are on his/her side and be willing to help him/her resist it. Ask him/her about seeking professional help. Both of you may need someone to walk alongside with you to seek freedom. Pornography often starts "small," but the person that begins using it will often seek more and more stimulation in hardcore pornography, and soon he/she will likely be addicted to it. This will affect your relationship, especially emotionally and sexually. Therefore, discuss with your partner about how you can help him/her.

Forgive. Everyone can make mistakes. Holding on to your partner's mistakes won't do anything good to either you or your partner. It makes you a bitter person. On the opposite, forgiveness sets you free. Forgiveness is once again a keyword in every relationship. Releasing forgiveness is important.

Set boundaries for the use of pornography. In consultation with your partner, set some boundaries in your home pertaining to the use of pornography. Do you need to have a screen free time after a certain time in the evening? Do you need to use filter to hinder access to websites with pornographic content? Whatever it is, try to set boundaries in agreement.

Open up for intimacy. As a start, you may not feel like having intimacy. That is OK. Give yourself some time. However, as the problem is dealt with, do open up for intimacy again with your partner.

Enjoy being together again by starting afresh. You may need to give it some time before sexual intimacy feels relaxed and natural, but if you both work on it, you may have a renewed sex life altogether.

"WHAT SHOULD I DO IF I STILL CAN'T BOUNCE BACK WITH MY PARTNER?"

You would need to remember that it takes time to rebound and arrive at greater intimacy, but it can be done. **If there is a will, there is a way**. The good news is that the relationship can be restored and go even deeper than before. The not so good news is that it will cost you both time and effort.

Many times when couples have come to seek help, we have realized that they believe that the counselor, therapist or coach will "fix" *their* marriage. They come with a "now I made it here so please fix my problems" kind of attitude, but that will never work. It is *always* the effort of the couple, with the *assistance* of the counselor/therapist/coach/God and/or other social support, that the broken relationship will be mended. So take the above steps, bit by bit, and don't hesitate seeking professional help if you can't seem to rebound. You are not alone, so be courageous and ask for help if you need it. Many others have been through similar problems, and many have found breakthroughs, so don't give up.

If your partner repeatedly continues to be unfaithful and has no intention to stop his/her involvement with other partners, you may want to consider going separate ways. We would say that the important thing is that you have done what you can do.

RELATIONSHIP BUILDERS

1. If you are the person that has committed infidelity or are stuck in pornography, take the courage to tell your partner, and follow the advice given in this chapter.

2. If you are the victim of infidelity or your partner is into pornography, be open to hearing your partner out and prepare yourself that things may be emotional and not so easy. However, don't lose heart but take one step at a time as you seek to bounce back.

POINTS TO PONDER

- Pornography will NOT improve sexual intimacy in your relationship.
- Comparison is the thief of joy.
- It is always better to be honest and expose problems in order for them to be solved.
- Anything kept in secret is hard to break free from. Bring your problem up by talking about it with someone bound by confidentiality.
- In the case of unfaithfulness, it is critical to cut off all ties with the one you have been unfaithful with.
- One of the keys to avoid unfaithfulness is to think about the right things.
- What you allow yourself to see, ponder or meditate on will be a starting point of your faithfulness to your partner.
- Forgiveness doesn't mean that you accept or approve what the other person did to you, but it does release you from being bound by it.
- What couples have overcome together will usually make their relationship stronger and deeper.

CHAPTER 6

RESPONSIBILITY

Meet your Partner's Needs with Love

Today, especially in the western world, we are living in societies where we frequently are very quick to claim our rights. We often demand our entitlement without responsibility. The danger is if this mentality creeps into a relationship. You demand your rights from your partner. He/she should be in a certain way and do certain things, but your own responsibility and part to play is not within the equation. In order for your relationship to not only work, but also constantly be growing and maturing, *responsibility* is a key component. **To take responsibility to nurture your partner is a significant ingredient in a happy relationship.**

"Maturity doesn't come with age, but with the acceptance of responsibility."[18] *– Edwin Louis Cole*

This statement can be applied not only to individuals, but to couples too. Just because a couple has been together for a very long time, that doesn't mean they have a mature relationship. **Rather, it is the level of responsibility to build and nurture that bond that brings the relationship to maturity**.

LIFE'S BUSYNESS CAN LEAD TO A STAGNATED RELATIONSHIP

The busyness of work, caring for children and home, concern for finances and other commitments often causes couples to lose the "spark" in their relationship, and causes it to stagnate, simply because the time is not spent to invest in one another. This is most common in the season when couples have small children. As such, when you have young kids, it is extra important to have some "couple's time", daily conversations and/or regular date nights (read more about this in chapter 2).

As **a relationship needs to grow and mature to continue to exist**, both parties need to take responsibility to cultivate the relationship on a regular basis. If someone claims that they always feel very much in love, year after year, decade after decade, and never feel a "dip" in his/her emotions for the other person, the person most likely doesn't tell the truth. **Every couple has "highs and lows" in their relationship**. However, we believe that when those "lows" come, it is crucial to stand on the *decision* made to love your partner. Even more so if you are married, a promise was made to love one another until death separates you. Look at this classical marriage vow:

"...To have and to hold from this day forward, for better or for worse, for richer, for poorer, in sickness and in health, to love and to cherish; from this day forward until death do us part."

Doesn't it sound like **you have to rely on "the decision of love" more than "the feeling of love"** in these kinds of circumstances?

CELEBRATE THE DIFFERENCES

Men and women are wired differently; probably no one would disagree with that. As a couple, **recognizing and celebrating one another's differences instead of trying to change our partner will create an atmosphere where teamwork can flourish** and both will be happy with who they are and what they are doing. We are designed to play different roles to complement each other, uniquely individual but yet complementing. It is of crucial value to take responsibility to find out what kind of person your true love really is; what are his/her needs, wants, fears, dreams, challenges and joys? Don't try to change him/her, but instead learn to appreciate and celebrate the differences.

THE 5 LOVE LANGUAGES

Love can be expressed through various means. One of the best ways to explain those expressions is made by Dr. Gary Chapman."[19] Dr. Chapman, who is a well-known author, describes how every person has a need to be loved, and that love can be communicated (given and received) in 5 various ways, namely through:

1. Words of affirmation

2. Physical touch

3. Quality time

4. Giving gifts

5. Acts of service

Every person has a primary love language, which is the way he/she feels that he/she is loved. Often we have more than one love language. The way we express our love to our partner is usually the love language that we ourselves feel loved by.

Dr. Chapman means that couples that don't communicate in the same lingo may face problems in their relationship, so we must **seek to express the love for our partner in the way that he/she feels loved**. The rule of thumb is to give what your partner wants instead of what you want to give him/her. And how do you know what your partner's love language is? There are two ways to find out: either you observe your partner, and/or you can ask him/her! Simply ask: "How do you feel loved the most?"

So what are the **5 love languages** all about? Briefly described, as we understand them:

1. Words of Affirmation

Words of affirmation include **speaking loving words** and verbally commenting things in order to make a person feel loved. This often builds confidence and trust in the relationship.

How do I express it?

Find out what your partner likes to hear to feel affirmed and loved and say it often. Compliment your spouse with heartfelt expressions such as *"I love you," "you look great in that skirt"* or *"you are the best husband in the world."* Let your partner feel you are totally for him/her.

2. Physical Touch

Physical touch is to express love through hugs, kisses, holding hands, sexual intimacy etc. This can be comforting and builds closeness in the relationship.

How do I express it?

Seek to **understand how your spouse likes to be touched**. It can be through a rubbing massage, or a brief kiss before going off to work (which actually does wonders). It could also be just a little touch on the back just above the waist when you are passing by your partner in your home. Sometimes just holding hands can make a couple feel really close. **Jim Coan, a psychologist and assistant professor in Neuroscience, did a study and found that** women under stress showed signs of immediate relief by only holding their husband's hand. **This seemed to be very effective when the woman was part of a satisfying marriage.**[20]

3. Quality Time

Quality time is simply to spend time to talk to and/or do activities together with your partner. This can help a couple to know one another on a deeper level and create greater unity as you find common interests. It also creates a platform with extensive time to communicate, a time to take interest in your partner's emotional wellbeing.

How do I express it?
We advise you to spend some time every day giving your partner **undivided attention** to share his/her heart and catch up on things. Be ready to share your views too. Go for a walk, play golf together or just have a cup of tea together at the kitchen table after the kids have gone to bed. One great way to have more quality time together, on top of those examples just given, is to **do house chores together**. Hanging the laundry or cooking together is a great way to find more time to connect.

Do ensure nothing steals your time you need to spend with your partner. When a couple has small children, it may be harder to spend quality time together. Our advice is to **take small moments here and there to communicate, if possible without interruptions**. You may consider having various kinds of quality time sessions. It could be a daily "quality time catch up" such as 10-15 minutes after dinner, sitting down over tea and talk, or in bed, if you're not too sleepy. I could be a biweekly or monthly dinner our or a yearly getaway, perhaps a retreat at a local hotel without the kids.

4. Giving Gifts
Giving gifts is to show love by buying things that the other person likes. This is a visible sign of your love and it shows your generosity and willingness to invest in the one you love. The other person feels appreciated and treasured. **Where your treasure is, there your heart will be as well**. If you want to stay long in a relationship, invest heavily in it!

How do I express it?
You can buy the classical things such as flowers or chocolate, but sometimes just getting inexpensive or even free gifts may work

just as well. The bottom-line is: be creative! (See more in chapter 7 for romantic tips.)

5. Acts of Service

Acts of service is to **serve the other person willingly and self-lessly as an expression of love** and with no expectation to receive acts of service in return. This is a practical way of showing love, which often results in that the partner feels truly loved and cared for as the thoughtful other partner inconveniences himself/herself for the other. This is one "cure" for a mundane relationship; a way to go against that selfishness that so many times sets in after years of being together.

How do I express it? It can be everything from taking out the garbage and folding clothes to buying the groceries or cooking the dinner. It could be something that is not done every day, such as giving your partner a footbath with massage or serving breakfast in bed. If you are a man: don't be afraid of being a gentleman. **Gentlemen are rare nowadays, but highly appreciated by many women**.

If you learn to master the 5 love languages discovered by Dr. Chapman, you are set for a great relationship. Sit down with your partner, talk about it, learn it and begin to apply it. Your **love can truly come ablaze** by following what you learn in this chapter.

THE TOP 5 EMOTIONAL NEEDS OF MEN AND WOMEN

As a couple, you need to keep "studying" the one you love. Pursue to understand what his/her likes and dislikes are, as well as needs, desires, dreams, strengths, weaknesses etc. Dr. Willard F. Harley, Jr. has stated the average Top 5 needs of men and the average top 5 needs of women.[21] This can help you and your partner to understand each other better as it paints a good picture of what an average man and an average woman actually needs. However, every couple is unique, so the needs may differ from couple to couple. As such, each couple should identify their own needs.

According to this study by Dr. Harley, the average **top five emotional needs of WOMEN** are:

1. Affection

According to Dr. Harley, **affection expresses care and brings security, protection, comfort and approval to the relationship**. With affection, a message is sent to the partner that *"I love you," "I will care for you,"* and *"You are important to me"*. **Without affection in the relationship, many women would feel disconnected from their husband**. Affection can be expressed with words, hugs, kisses, holding hands, giving gifts etc., and it has nothing to do with sex. Harley says that the "typical male" sees affection as foreplay to sex, while women don't. Therefore, men should seek to show affection on a regular basis without any intention for sex. As a man, you may not always *feel* in love with your woman, but **making her feel loved is a *choice***. So be lavish in showing affection to your woman. She'll love it!

2. Conversation

At the early stage of most relationship there is a lot of conversation going on. Someone jokingly said that *"In the first year of marriage, the man speaks and the wife listens. In the second year, the woman speaks and the husband listens. In the third year, they both speak and the neighbors listen."* Hopefully this is not true in your relationship. But the point is, as years goes by, there is a risk that you both will communicate less, *unless* you consciously make it a point to communicate regularly with each other.

Create moments of relaxed conversations around the dinner table, when you do your house chores and even when you are apart during the day. My husband and I (Marie) still call one another several times every day. We send each other text messages, expressing our love for one another as well as just talking about what is in our heart at that moment. We basically didn't stop that habit since courtship days. We just love to talk and be together. If you don't do that today, it is not too late to start! Try sending one text message to just express love to your partner. A loving expression like that can make wonders!

Dr. Harley further says that **the most satisfying conversation is one that has a focus on getting to know one other, showing an interest in each other, and discussing topics of interest to both**. He also states that the average woman needs 15 hours of quality conversation per week.

Create opportunities, despite your busyness, to invest in your partner through heart-to-heart conversations. As a man, remember that most women love to talk and share what's on their mind. Showing a woman genuine interest and paying undivided attention to her makes her blossom. She will love the feeling of a good quality conversation with you.

Be an attentive listener as well as a ready speaker. It is equally important to listen with focus, as it is to be willing to open up and share things.

3. Honesty and Openness

According to Dr. Harley, a sense of security is "the bright golden thread woven through all of a woman's five basic needs... **To feel secure, a wife must trust her husband to give her accurate information about his past, the present, and the future.**" This is where honesty and openness comes in. We have shared earlier about the "open book policy" and how it creates security and trust in your relationship. So as the boyfriend/husband; try to be as transparent as you can with your girlfriend/wife; it will make her feel more secure in your relationship.

4. Financial Support

As mentioned in the previous point, feeling secure is very important for a woman, and there is often an unspoken expectation that the man will take the main responsibility for the finances, especially a family's finances. Finances are a common area for quarrels, disagreements and frictions and often cause stress among couples. Why do you think ladies, in many parts of the world, still want to marry a financially secure man? Likewise it is also common in some parts of the world that parents will not approve a relationship or marriage unless the man has a stable and good income.

5. Commitment to the Family

The 5th top need of women is a commitment to the family. Building a happy and strong family unit is a natural instinct for the average woman. **Many women prefer that the man take on the role of a responsible leader and a great father.** As such, there is often an expectation on the man to willingly spend time with the children by playing with them as well as teach and impart things to them on a regular basis. It may also involve undivided time spent on family gatherings or outings. Many women in particular appreciate when her man takes interest in her extended family, such as keeping in contact with her parents and taking time off meeting extended family and relatives. If you are a married man, you are ultimately responsible for your family – your family's wellbeing as a whole. As a husband and father, do your utmost to keep your promises; especially when it comes to family time.

Now, let's take a look at what Dr. Willard F. Harley, Jr. states as the average **Top 5 emotional needs of MEN**:

1. Sexual Fulfillment

This is the strongest need of the average man, which may be difficult to understand for women, in the same way that men may not understand women's need for affection. Just like the husband should seek to give his wife much affection, the wife should seek to meet the husband's sexual need. Be available for sexual intimacy, but also take initiative for it.

2. Recreational Companionship

The need to laugh and have fun with your partner is the second top need for men according to Harley's study. Just like you most likely had lots of fun in your courtship days, **you need to have fun after you say, "I do" too**, and this is especially important for men. Harley means that **doing enjoyable things together is vital to the marriage**. He says, "Men place surprising importance on having their wives as recreational companions." As a woman, set aside time to do enjoyable things together with your partner. It may be sacrificing other things that you would prefer doing, but it may be worth investing that time and effort, as it would meet a need in your partner as well as enrich the relationship. Follow your partner on a round of golf or join him for his favorite sports game or movie. It'll be a great opportunity to meet his need of companionship and you can have loads of fun together.

3. An Attractive Spouse

Dr. Harley's research also concluded that a man feels good when he looks at his attractive and beautiful woman. Most men don't only appreciate a woman's inner qualities alone, but take pride in a beautiful and good-looking partner.

As a wife/woman, look your best for your husband/man. Don't become shapeless and ignorant about how you look, but put in that little extra effort to look good, whether it means to exercise, lose weight, buy some new clothes or put on makeup. So don't argue and say things like, "if he loves me, he has to accept me the way I am." In a way yes, but the point is to make the best out of what you are and not be careless about your body or your looks, as it matters to a man. Building a relationship is about meeting one another's needs in love. So if you love your man, aim to be attractive in the sight of your man.

4. Domestic Support

Most men appreciate peace and quietness, so one of the worst things a woman can do when her man comes home after a long day at work is to start nagging at him, blaming him for various things. You probably heard; *"better to live in the desert than with a quarrelsome and nagging wife."* **Many men have a need of a peaceful and harmonious home** where the female creates a homely atmosphere in the house and ensures the daily matters runs smooth. He also has a need that his woman takes care of him by offering him support. In many societies today, majority of men and women share the responsibilities at home because both of them works outside the home. Hence, it is good to talk about what each one is responsible for and what responsibilities are to be shared.

5. Admiration/Respect

He needs her to be proud of him. Admiration gives motivation and energy to the man. He needs admiration for "the now;" for who he is today and not what he could potentially become in the future.

Men often become defensive when they are criticized, but if encouraged, men can be empowered to be more confident and as such also become greater achievers.

Someone once said that to disrespect your husband's choices again and again is like pricking him again and again with little pins. Ladies, are you provoking your partner? If he feels disrespected, he may withdraw from you. But the opposite is also true; **if you talk to and treat your man with respect, he would want to draw closer to you**, share his heart with you, and as such, your relationship grows more intimate. If things go wrong sometimes when your husband made a certain decision, remember that he is learning. **Don't correct him**. Even if you disagree with him, do not dismiss his ideas. Trust your man.

Ladies, do consider:

- Be trusting instead of controlling.

- Be grateful instead of complaining.

- Be respectful instead of demeaning.

Do remember that what you say and how you look at your partner can make him feel like a hero or like a total failure.

> *"Respect a man, he will do the more"* – James Howell

CHANGE STARTS WITH YOURSELF

Don't wait for your partner to change and don't ever try to change him/her; but take responsibility by starting with yourself, as you are the only one you can change. Be willing to change yourself for the benefit of your partner, but let your partner be responsible for his/her own change. You are only responsible for your own behavior and attitude in the relationship. **Focus on your own assignment; not your partner's**. For why would you look at the speck in your partner's eye, but not consider the plank in your own?

We recall a coaching session we had with a man in his fifties. He had asked to speak to us about his relationship problem. In the first session, when asked what he perceived was the problem at hand, he took up a piece of paper from his pocket and said: "I will tell you what the problem is." He started to read from a list with all the weaknesses of his partner, how she was like and what she did and did not do. When he was done with his many points, we said to him: "OK. Now that we have gotten to know more about your wife, please tell us about yourself? What are your weaknesses?" The man got stunned and couldn't come up with anything, because according to him, it was all *her* issues that caused the relationship problems. So even after trying to help him to see that both parties plays a role in the success of a relationship, he still wouldn't want to accept it or acknowledge it. **So we knew by experience that we would not be able to help him any further.**

The point here is to always change us first, and change in our partner's life many times follow suit. But don't change yourself only so that your partner will change; change yourself because it is a goal in itself. **Place yourself under the magnifying glass before finding fault in others**. The optimum is of course that both of you **work as a team**, where you both continually recognize and respect one another's differences, needs and wants, and do what you can to meet those needs joyfully and without grumbling or comparing.

HOW DO WE SAFEGUARD OUR RELATIONSHIP?

Anything of value deserves to be safeguarded and protected, and that includes your love relationship. When needs are not met in the marriage for a prolonged period of time, it is not rare that an affair will occur.

When a woman seeks a partner outside of marriage, it is often someone that shows her attention and affection, while for the man it is many times about meeting the need of sexual fulfillment. In both cases, this is in line with the top needs of the respective gender that have been unmet. So we can see that as a couple, **it is of utmost importance to find out what your partner's top needs are and to do your best to fulfill those needs**. This is one powerful way to safeguard the marriage.

Some other tips to safeguard your relationship (except this entire book!) is to say NO to the following:

- Secrets

- Pornography

- Close exclusive friendships with the opposite sex

These things can bring strong temptations and eventually lead to an affair; something that most people will regret later. Once again, it is about taking responsibility for the relationship not only to work out, but also to be happy and last for a lifetime!

IN CONCLUSION

Men and women often have different needs. **For a love relationship to flourish and come ablaze, both parties should aim to meet the needs of the other.** It's pretty common that most people like to help others in great need, but so often the need of our partner is forgotten. As you take responsibility to make your partner's life a little better each day, you desire a great thing, and you will be able to see your relationship move to another level. **A couple needs to understand that they are to complement and complete one another; not compete with each other.** Each one is responsible to give of oneself for the sake of benefiting the other. That is exactly how an outstanding relationship is built! **When you start to take responsibility with actions, things will begin to change**! Action will always bring reaction! Investing in your partner by finding out his/her needs, and then willingly and creatively meeting those needs, will usually cause a very positive response from your partner and with that, **your love relationship can come ablaze.**

RELATIONSHIP BUILDERS:

1. Find out what your partner's primary and secondary love languages are, by first   observing your partner, trying out some of the above expressions of the love languages, and then ask your partner for confirmation of your conclusion.

2. Write down two practical ways to "speak" those primary and secondary love   languages of your partner and then put them into practice within this week.

3. Go through the top 5 needs of men and women respectively, together as a couple, if possible. Rank them in order of importance to you and discuss which needs are strongly met, and which needs you need to give more attention to. Share with your partner.

4. Commit to showing love according to your partner's love language on a regular basis as well as meeting the top needs as often as it is appropriate.

POINTS TO PONDER

- Responsibility to nurture your partner is a significant ingredient in a happy relationship.
- Rely more on the *decision* of love rather than the *feeling* of love.
- Every couple has "highs" and "lows" in their relationship, just make sure the highs outweigh the lows.
- A rule of thumb: give your partner what he/she needs; not what you want to give to him/her.
- Give your partner the affection due to him/her.
- Where your treasure is, there your heart will be also. Your heart will follow your investment, so invest wisely into your relationship.
- Clear goals for your relationship will diminish tension.
- Remove the plank in your own life before working on your partner's speck.
- As a couple, you are complementing and completing each other; not competing with each other.
- Responsibility with actions creates change.

CHAPTER 7

ROMANCE

How to Create a Romantic Relationship

Chemistry alone is not enough to make a relationship last for a lifetime. One of the things that are significant for a stable and lasting love relationship is romance.

REGULAR DATING

Dating is usually to be involved with someone in a romantic way. When you first met your loved one, you were most likely spending everything from a few weeks to a few years to date one another before moving on to deeper levels of engagement or marriage. **Regular dating is an essential ingredient to a strong marriage/relationship**. Keep on dating the one you love throughout your life.

It is good to consider having a "once a week date night" for you and your partner. If you can't commit to once a week, aim to date at least once biweekly or monthly. It may be challenging, especially the moment you get married and have kids, but it is good for you! You may need to really **plan to set aside time to date**; especially if you are parents of young children, who will take up a lot of your time and attention. To find a good babysitter is likely going to be worth the money and effort. If you nurture your relationship by taking time off for dating, your relationship can blossom even under this busy season of your lives.

SHOW LITTLE ACTS OF LOVE DAILY

On top of dating your partner on a regular basis, **doing daily small little acts of love throughout the day will build the**

relationship. Those small acts of love could be things such as kissing your partner goodbye before leaving the house in the morning, and doing the same as you meet again in the evening. Send a few text messages throughout the day telling your partner that you love him/her; that you were thinking about him/her etc. **Whatever you commit to on a daily basis will make a big difference in the long run.** Whatever you do habitually becomes part of your character. **Aim to live every day of your life as if it was your last day.** Do meaningful things to add romance and value to your relationship.

MORE A COMMITMENT THAN A FEELING

The truth is that **romance is of crucial value for a love relationship to stay happy, healthy and harmonious**. To build a lasting relationship, you need to continually invest and sow into it. It is more a commitment than a feeling. Commitment anticipates that the relationship is going to be permanent. It's a conscious decision to direct one's affection to someone else. **Feelings come and go, but a commitment is a commitment, and if seen as such, the relationship can last "until death do you part."** Your feelings towards each other *will* go up and down; sometimes you may feel so in love that you have butterflies in your stomach, and sometimes you might feel that your relationship is very mundane and dull, or even wonder how it would be like to live with someone else. In times when things are not on the "high" in between you, **your commitment to one another will be the determining factor for you to keep going together.** And remember, in these seasons, you will need to "water" your relationship more consciously.

52 TIPS FOR BOOSTING ROMANCE IN YOUR RELATIONSHIP

Romance requires some planning, time and effort, but giving room for it in your relationship is a wise move. **Romance is all about**

going the extra mile for your partner. *"But hey, I am not that romantic kind of person..."* No worries, everyone can learn or re-learn to be romantic. Like many other things in a relationship, it is a choice you can make. It's worth the effort, as romance can be pretty fun and will add flavor to your relationship!

Here are 52 tips that you can consider doing to boost the romance in your relationship. These 52 tips can last you for a whole year if you commit to one tip every week.

1. Buy a bouquet of roses on an ordinary day.

2. Prepare morning coffee and cut out a sandwich in a heart shape for breakfast.

3. Write a love letter.

4. Cook a three-course dinner at home on a weekday night (preferably homemade).

5. Arrange a candle light evening with heart to heart sharing, nuts and drinks.

6. Drive your partner to the top of a mountain at night, sit at the cliff and watch the scenery together.

7. Meet up in the park for a picnic.

8. Write a love poem, cut them into pieces and send it in the mail to your partner.

9. Prepare a bubble bath for your partner with aromatic oils (or book a couple spa session).

10. Buy a trophy for your partner with a script such as "to the most outstanding partner in the world."

11. Write "I love you forever" on the bathroom mirror with soap or lipstick.

12. Pick wild flowers for your partner from the field or road-side.

13. Watch a romantic movie together.

14. Make a huge greeting card out of a shoebox or similar, and glue pictures, stickers and lots of text, expressing your love and affection.

15. Book a surprise weekend for two to an interesting and romantic destination.

16. Ask your partner out for a date unexpectedly in the middle of the week.

17. Send flowers to your partner's work place.

18. Bring your partner for a breakfast buffet at an exclusive hotel.

19. Call a radio station and dedicate a love song to your partner. Send a text message that says he/she must tune in to that radio channel at that specific time.

20. Buy a frame and put in a photo of the both of you from one of your first dates or first year together. Wrap it up in shiny wrapping paper.

21. Spread rose petals all around the bedroom.

22. Buy a small surprise gift (such as your partner's favorite chocolate or perfume, some new clothes, a designer pen or a packet of gourmet tea).

23. Give your partner a footbath: a basin with warm water and some oil. Have towel, foot file and foot cream handy, and give your partner a good foot massage.

24. Wink unexpectedly at your partner when in public.

25. Make a heart shaped bookmark and place it in your partner's book.

26. Kiss your partner's hand graciously by lowering your lips to the level of his/her hand.

27. Bake your partner's favorite cake.

28. Dance in the living room.

29. Watch the sunset together.

30. Make a lunchbox for your partner with his favorite food.

31. Take a happy "selfie" photo together and put it into a frame.

32. Write a loving post on Facebook to declare your love publicly and tag your partner.

33. Give your partner a good neck massage after a hard days' work.

34. Toast each other when you sit down for dinner and say some unexpected loving words to your partner in front of the family/friends around the table.

35. Surprise your partner with breakfast in bed on a rainy Saturday morning.

36. Compose a song and sing it for your partner.

37. Make a list of the top ten things you appreciate and love about your partner, write it nicely on a card and pass to him/her.

38. Take a carriage trip around the city.

39. Send a written invitation in the mail for something special such as a concert or a visit to the theater.

40. Prepare a cheese tray with crackers and two hot cups of tea. Light some candles for a romantic atmosphere.

41. Give an unforeseen compliment.

42. Arrange a midweek movie night away from the children for just the two of you.

43. Do the laundry or dishes together while planning your next holiday together.

44. Book a hotel night with your partner for the reason that you just want to be together.

45. Place a love note in your partner's phone case or wallet.

46. Call your partner from work without any other reason than to say "I love you."

47. Comb your partner's hair and give a good scalp massage.

48. Write small notes as clues where one note leads to the other, and then have a room prepared for romance…

49. Prepare a speech on a Monday morning breakfast table in front of the kids to express your love and gratitude for your partner.

50. Go to an Amusement Park or the Zoo, only the two of you, holding hands and eating ice cream like in the courtship days.

51. Wake up early to watch the sunrise together at some lovely spot, while sipping morning coffee together.

52. Record a video message of yourself telling your partner how much you love and appreciate him/her and send it to him/her.

These are just examples and ideas that hopefully can stir your own creativity. Let inspiration flow and start being romantic!

KEEP PURSUING ONE ANOTHER

All relationships have their hills and their valleys, but by adding romance to your relationship, the valleys can become hilltops again. **Romance is about pursuing one another again and again.** As such, you would need to keep pursuing (chasing after) one another throughout your lives. That is how the relationship wouldn't only be maintained, but purposefully grow deeper.

FILL UP EACH OTHER'S "LOVE CONTAINER"

Perhaps you feel like your relationship is going down the drain and has been dashed against the hard ground of reality. The closeness is no longer there and reality is more like solitary confinement than intimate closeness. So many individuals in a relationship are feeling that they have grown apart; their relationship has come to a halt. The fact is every human has a need to be loved. It is really damaging to your health if you are not being loved or feeling loved and cared for by someone. It has been proven that love can prolong someone's life, it can make recovery from sickness faster and it can transform any individual mentally.

Imagine your partner having a tank, a **"love container"**, pretty much like a car has a gas tank. It constantly needs to be filled up. If you are running your car on low, a warning sign goes on. Likewise, there may be warning signs if your partner's love container is running low. Your romance and love might have come to a halt for the very same reason a car stops when having an empty tank. You have forgotten to fill up each other's love container. Like you regularly fill up your car, you need to fill each other's love container repeatedly by constantly expressing your love for one another in words and actions.

IS THE SPARK GONE?

If you have lost that initial spark in your relationship, you need to go back to your **first works.** Think about what you did during courtship days. Likely you did meet his/her needs back then, but as time goes by, it's easy to start neglecting it. Our advice is to do what you did when you were head over heels in love with your partner. Think about what you did and just do it again. It could be taking your partner out for a candlelight dinner. It could be hugging and kissing one another every time you meet or say goodbye. It could be calling your partner sweet names such as *"Darling"* or *"Honey"*, or just saying *"I love you"* every day. Initially you may not *feel* like it, but remember, if you would like to get back that first feeling, you must invest and do what you first did when you started out your relationship. **Therefore, revisit the first works of love.** If the spark wasn't there at all, you may want to consider the 52 romantic tips mentioned above. They will definitely help to bring happiness and romance into your relationship. Even though they may feel "mechanic" as a start, as time goes by, they can really help change the feelings for your partner and light the spark.

TAKE CARE OF ONE ANOTHER'S HEARTS

You need to take care of one another's hearts before someone else does. If you don't do that, the road downhill is inevitable. Always seek to win your partner's love, in the same way you did when you were dating him/her, and let the love grow deeper. Treat his/her heart with tender care. Then you'll have all odds to have a love relationship that will grow deep and last for a lifetime.

ENJOY YOUR LIFE JOURNEY TOGETHER

Life is short on this earth. As such, don't sweat the small stuff; don't pay attention to petty issues. As you both grow older, keep enjoying your life journey together. Someone once said, *"An archaeologist is the best husband a woman can have; the older she gets, the more interested he is in her."* It is meant to be a joke, but there is an important point here. **Your love and interest can and should increase as the years and decades goes by.** White hair, a round stomach or wrinkles doesn't matter so much; when the two of you have travelled such a long way together, hopefully you have built such intimacy that it goes far beyond that. You have a friendship and deep love that makes you cohesive as one "unit", far beyond just romance. Isn't it touching when you see a really old couple that still lovingly holds hands in public?

LAUGH TOGETHER

Keep having fun together and laugh often, even as you grow older. I (Marie) remember my old grandparents sitting in the garden at my parent's place one summer afternoon, and how my grandpa suddenly said to the people gathered around the table: *"Last week, Maj* (my grandma) *bought a new bathing suit. It was patterned with fish. But when Maj put it on, it became big sharks!"* My grandma laughed and everyone laughed. They knew one another so well so they also knew how they could joke with one another without giving offense. **That is the beauty of sticking to**

the same person for long. Laughter can heal; so if you haven't laughed lately as a couple, watch a comedy or do something really fun that can get you to laugh together. It can work wonders.

RELATIONSHIP BUILDERS:

1. Make use of the 52 romantic tips list by committing to (minimum) one tip per week. Vary between the simple and the more advanced tips, or simply come up with your own! The idea is to build in romance into your relationship.

2. Find things you enjoy doing together and commit to spend the time to do them, even when you're busy or stressed. Plan one event for the following week.

3. If you need a baby sitter, now is the time to source one so you can have regular dating time.

POINTS TO PONDER

- Regular dating is an essential ingredient to a strong marriage/relationship.
- Build your relationship daily by doing small little acts of love throughout the day.
- Commitment is a determining factor for you to keep going together for long.
- If you have lost the spark in your relationship, go back to the first works of love.
- It probably takes less than 5 minutes a day to be romantic. Be it!
- Romance is about pursuing one another again and again.
- Take care of one another's hearts before someone else do.
- Laughter can heal and work wonders. Have a good laugh together.
- Don't sweat the small stuff.
- Distance in a relationship is not measured in miles but in affection.

CHAPTER 8

ROUTE CLARITY

Define Core Values and Goals for a Happier Future

Whether you are dating, planning for marriage or have been in a relationship for a long time, route clarity will help you move your relationship in the right direction. Furthermore, you will be able to avoid lots of conflicts if you are working on defining common goals in your relationship.

MAKE ROOM FOR ROUTE CLARITY CONVERSATIONS

It is important to **make time for conversations about mutual core values and future goals.** It's good for a relationship to have route clarity. Some call it purpose or vision. **Route clarity is to define where you are going in life** – what your core values and future goals are. Where are you heading in your relationship? Do not let your relationship just drift aimlessly; then it will likely end up on shallow ground. Instead, have clear goals, visions and dreams for your relationship. You can even write them down, and put them up on the wall as a reminder. If you see it and confess it, you will be heading in that direction. We started about 10 years ago with what we call a **"vision board"** and have encouraged other couples to do the same. A vision board is a big photo frame with photos/pictures/text or other things that reminds you about what you want to see in your life together. It will keep you focused, and chances for you to experience its fulfillment is great.

WHAT ARE CORE VALUES?

Core values are the fundamental beliefs a person has; they are strong convictions of something that aims to guide and determine every decision, behavior and action of that person. Core values can help people to know what is right and what is wrong; they assist the person to make the correct choices in life, according to the values he/she holds, and becomes the kind of life you will live. Some core values are your personal ones; but if you are in a relationship, it is important to **define some of the core values in relation to and in agreement with your partner**, especially when it comes to things pertaining to your relationship and your family life.

EXAMPLES OF MUTUAL CORE VALUES

As you spend time to clarify your route together as a couple, here are some examples of core values to help you get started:

- A belief that family is of fundamental importance.

- A conviction that saying sorry is always the best policy.

- A belief that doing your best is crucial.

- A conviction that God needs a central place in your daily life.

- A conviction to live in truth and honesty without exceptions.

- A belief in having a healthy lifestyle.

Core values can also be defined with one word, such as:

- Loyalty

- Honesty

- Commitment

- Positivity

- Love

- Generosity

As you write down your core values, it is good that each one of you do it individually first, and then come into agreement of the top five (or how many you would want to have) that can be your mutual core values. As these values have been identified and written down, you may also want to write down future goals that are time sensitive.

WHAT IS A DREAM RELATIONSHIP OR MARRIAGE TO YOU?

In order for you to progress in the right direction in your relationship, it is vital to know where you are going with it. **Without a sense of knowing where you are going, as mentioned, you will most likely drift randomly and end up on a shallow**. So our tip here is that both of you sit down separately and think through what a dream relationship would look like, what would it encompass? How would you treat each other? Here you just dream and write it down on a piece of paper. It could be things such as, *"A dream relationship is filled with kisses and hugs"*, *"A dream relationship is to have sex every day"*, *"A dream relationship is to be able to communicate openly with each other"*, and *"A dream relationship is having a lot of money"*. Just dream on and write it down.

After the both of you have done this exercise, you can sit down together and look at each other's lists and try to find some common ones or some that are almost alike. Write those down on a separate piece of paper. **Pick at least five and then seek to agree that this is what you both would like to see in your dream relationship**. Now you have some goals to work towards that you both agree on in your relationship and you will not just drift randomly. Discuss what you need to do to achieve this, either together or separately.

FUTURE GOALS

While core values have to do with your inner life: beliefs and character, your future goals have more to do with practical things you would like to see/achieve. Write your individual lists first, share them with one another and then agree on the top three or five. Some example of future goals could be:

- Buy a house within XX years of marriage.

- Plan to have XX children within the span of XX years.

- One of you to stay home with the children until they are XX years old.

- Bring your elderly parents for a long trip to another continent once every five years.

- Save up XX amount of cash yearly to purchase XX in XX years' time.

- Give XX amount of money to a welfare organization by a certain time.

By doing this you avoid lots of unnecessary arguments. As both of you have agreed on your future goals, both of you should align to those agreements and shouldn't argue otherwise. A piece of advice: **aim towards having measurable goals**. Meaning, you should be able to measure your progress and be able to know once the goals are reached. **It's a great feeling when both of you have worked together towards something and achieved it.**

GETTING YOU STARTED

As you embark on your route clarity journey, there are a few things we suggest you discuss as early as possible in your relationship. Even if you've been together or married for long, you may want to revisit some of these steps and see if there are things that you both can improve (and we are sure there are, because we can always improve things in our relationships!):

What are the expectations each one will have of the other in the relationship? Discuss things like how much time to be spent together weekly, work life balance, time off for dating and intimacy etc.

Baby planning. When would you both want to start trying for a baby and how many children would you desire to have?

When the first baby arrives. Does one of you need to stay at home or work less? At what age will the baby/child be sent to daycare/school? Are there other childcare alternatives?

Where are you going to keep your money? Will you have a joint account, individual savings or both? We advise that you join at least one account once you get married, unless one partner has gambling problems or serious spending issues. It is good to agree on a certain percentage or amount of your individual salaries that will go into the joint account for house expenses, car expenses, holidays etc. We have found that **a joint account for a majority of your income will lessen the risk of quarrels over finances**, which is a very common reason for marriage tensions and even divorce.

How are you going to spend your money? What is appropriate? Will you give donations to charity on a regular basis? How many percent will you save each month? How much can you spend on various things? **To make a monthly and/or yearly budget is strongly advisable**.

Here, we have found that **transparency is a key**. Give each other freedom, but be transparent when it comes to bigger amounts. The two of you should agree what works best for you. A recommendation from many financial advisers is that you should aim to save/invest about 15% of your income.

What are the values that you hold on to? Speaking the truth, taking shared responsibility for household chores and children, respect when communicating, and not quarrel in front of the children...? The list can be long. Don't only briefly discuss these, but write them down, commit them to memory and start to live by them. Some advice is to put your family values, which you have agreed on, on your refrigerator, so that everyone in the family can see them, just to remind yourselves what you live by and aim towards.

It could be something like this:

In our family...

- We speak the truth in love

- We respect one another and one another's belongings

- We help each other willingly (etc.)

Faith/Religion matters. Will you be creating a habit of praying at the table and/or at bedtime? Do you value going to church or attending other religious gatherings on a weekly basis? Are you going to raise your children in the same faith?

Health matters. Is it important for you to eat healthy and impart that to your kids? Is sweet stuff allowed on weekdays? Are you going to create habits of exercise and outdoor activities for your children? If yes, how often?

How do you spend your time? Is it important for you to spend time with parents and in-laws? How often should they be visited?

How much "me-time" do you feel you need (for example evenings out without your partner, spent alone or with your friends?)

When it comes to work and career, how much is acceptable when it comes to working overtime and traveling for business?

How do you want to raise your children? This includes things such as expressing love, discipline, house rules, study time versus playtime etc. You might ask yourself if this is necessary. Yes, if you would like to avoid unnecessary arguments and conflicts. But of course, adjustments can be made along the way, but the foundational things should be discussed.

The keywords here are preparation and progression. Prepare as much as you can and keep talking about whatever comes up. Your common goal is to progress in your relationship. We remember a couple we helped that was totally devastated when their newborn baby didn't sleep in the night it and caused great tension in their relationship. We asked them what they had expected. But they hadn't read a single book; neither tried to prepare themselves by gaining knowledge about what to expect with a newborn baby. **Preparation is crucial to avoid surprises and for progression to take place.**

PAINTING THE SMALL AND THE BIG PICTURE

As you discuss and clarify your route as a couple/family, you can also divide your future goals into long-term and short-term goals. For example, a long-term goal in the area of finances could be to give an ongoing monthly donation of $ XX to a certain charity and to save XX% of the monthly income, while a short-term goal could be that from January to June in a particular year, there would be a need to save up $ XX for a certain upcoming expense (discuss *how* you are going to save; such as cutting cost by eating out only once a week instead of five times a week etc.)

RELATIONSHIP BUILDERS:
1. Set aside an hour or two to think through and write down your own personal core values and future goals for your dream relationship/marriage.

2. Discuss with your partner what values you currently are holding on to or what you wrote down, and what you think could become core values in your life as well as agree on relationship goals.

3. Set aside another time a few days later, where both of you discuss and write down a list of at least 3 mutual core values and at least 3 mutual future goals for your dream relationship.

4. Follow up with a conversation one week later and see if you would want to amend the list. If yes, make the changes; if no, start to live by your new values and goals. **As your route as a couple/family is clarified, it will help you to focus and build your future in the same direction!**

5. Create your own vision board and set it up so you constantly see it and remind yourselves about it.

POINTS TO PONDER

- Route clarity is to define where you are going in life.
- Defining mutual core values and future goals will eliminate unnecessary arguments and conflicts.
- A vision is a picture of the future. It will bring you from where you are to where you want to be in your relationship. Have a vision you agree on.
- A relationship without a vision will drift until it stops on a shallow.
- Aim towards having measurable goals.
- Consider saving at least 15% of what you earn.

CHAPTER 9

REFLECTION

A Key Ingredient in your Relationship

THE POWER OF REFLECTION

Reflection is probably one of the most neglected activities in our high-speed society today. Everything is expected to happen without delay; fast food, high-speed Internet, photos at an instant, "speed-dating" etc.

Oxford Dictionary defines reflection as "serious thought or consideration." Life in the fast lane doesn't give room for reflection. But **reflection is extremely important for every aspect of a person's life**, and particularly when you are in a relationship. Reflection is to stop what you are doing, and take some time to think about your life from various aspects, basically **to ponder your ways**. You can take a moment (a minute or two) to reflect on what was being said in a conversation earlier, or you can take an evening (a few hours) to reflect on your marriage, your work, your own character or your life goals (it can be basically anything).

THE PURPOSE OF REFLECTION

The purpose is to seriously think about and consider your ways in order to possibly improve certain things. **You can use reflection to make profound and positive changes in your life**. Reflection is "self-care." It means you take some time off for yourself to evaluate your life, get some self-insight, deal with your own weaknesses and rejoice over your own successes etc. It is a time for you to be alone and consider your life.

THE PROCESS OF REFLECTION

Find a place of solitude. When you want to reflect, it should be done in a place where you won't be disturbed or distracted. You could go for a walk in the forest, sit on a quiet beach in the early morning or spend time in a closed-door bedroom.

Look back on your past. Think through your happy or sad moments of the past. Are there any concerns regarding your past? Here you may need to deal with certain issues such as anger, shame and guilt. Are there any people you need to release forgiveness to? Do you need to forgive yourself? Were there certain choices you made that led to certain events? What have you learnt from those experiences? What are the good things you can rejoice over? What are the successes you want to celebrate and be thankful for? Take a pen and write your reflections down in a journal. Remember, the more emotionally healthy you are, the easier it will be to deal with relationship issues.

Look at the now. Where are you at right now? Are you happy in your relationship? Are your attitudes towards the love relationship you are in positive? Grateful? Unselfish? Is your work satisfactory? Do you need to let go of certain things or people in your life? How do you spend your time? Are you where you want to be physically? Emotionally? Financially? Socially? Spiritually?

Look at the future in the light of the past and the now. What are the current things in your life you would want to change? Consider some solutions to change certain things and write them down, preferably in "step by step form" and within a time frame. What are some future goals that you have? What do you need to do to get there?

Reflect on a regular basis. It is good to take time now and then to reflect on your life: to ponder your ways, learn from mistakes and set goals for the future to achieve a desired change. As you build in this special habit in your life, you will likely become a better person, and that will improve your love relationship too. Reflect together as a couple as well. Are you still on the route that you decided on or are you deviating? What are your feelings about your relationship? Is it getting stronger or weaker? Do you need to work on some areas? What can be done? You see, if couples could do this regularly, they could easily avoid a negative development in their relationship.

THE CONNECTION BETWEEN SELF-CARE AND TOLERATING YOUR PARTNER

There is often a direct connection between self-care and your level of tolerance for your partner. When you find yourself losing patience with your partner, or you begin to feel that small matters that your partner says or does irritates you a lot, you should probably do a "temperature check." Ask yourself the following questions:

- *"Have I neglected taking some time off for myself?"* You may just need to sleep in, take a walk or go out to some quiet and serene place for solitude. When was the last time you went out with your mates? Had a coffee with your friends?

- *"Do I have any underlying issues that I have not dealt with?"* If there are issues such as anger or unforgiveness from a previous offense, it needs to be dealt with.

It is important to protect your own heart, to **love yourself and take time to reflect on your life**. You may even need to speak to a friend or counselor to support you and help you sort out certain things in your life. Remember, you consist of body, soul and spirit, and all three parts need attention and care. Balance is the key to a healthy life.

DEFINE YOUR RESPONSIBILITY

Work on your own character; not your partner's. **It is not your responsibility to "fix" your partner; neither is it your partner's responsibility to "fix" or change you**. Take full responsibility for your own feelings and emotions, character and behavior. You can only change yourself. When you change for the better in your own character and behavior, you will affect your partner's response in a positive way too.

PRACTICAL SOLUTIONS: "THE WHAT AND THE HOW"

Ask yourself on a regular basis: "What do I think my partner wants me to change?" Then write it down and **work on changing one thing at the time**. I give you an example. Your partner has been asking you to spend more time with him/her as you've been working and stayed very late in the office lately. He/she also felt you are often distracted by many things when communicating at home. Take some solitude time, find some potential solutions and write them down. The list could contain two columns: "the what" (defining the issue) and "the how" (your action plan).

THE BEST GIFT

One of the best gifts you could ever give your partner is that **you yourself are emotionally and mentally whole**. That means you have dealt with major issues from your past or current life, such as envy, jealousy, anger and insecurity. For example, if you are insecure because you've been betrayed in a previous relationship, and you find it really hard to trust your partner, you may become suspicious and end up controlling your partner, which will not add anything good to your relationship. Trust takes time to build, so you may need to explain to your partner that you face this issue, but there comes a time when you should be able to overcome it and fully trust again; or at least not be controlling. As such, **take**

regular time to care for yourself through reflection and following actions so that you can become the optimal partner for your loved one. He/she will be happier and you will be happier with yourself too.

A word of caution here: if you have been coming out of a broken relationship and would like to enter another, make sure you have been healed and overcome your old relationship. Otherwise you will bring in resentment, anger, and all kinds of emotions into your new relationship. One way we can find out whether a person is ready for a new relationship could be as simple as asking him/her about his/her previous relationship and partner. If he/she can't speak of the relationship or person without reacting with anger or other negative emotions, we pretty much know he/she is not ready. **The way you leave often determines the way you enter. What goes around comes around.**

RELATIONSHIP BUILDERS:

1. Set aside one hour this week to practice reflection.

2. Write down your reflections: your thoughts and your possible action plans (you can buy a notebook and dedicate it for your reflections).

POINTS TO PONDER

- Consider your ways and the direction of your relationship, so you know how to navigate correctly.
- Ponder the path you are on and make a turn if you need. You choose which way to go.
- Always bear in mind this question: "What do I think my partner wants me to change in my life?"
- Don't always look for faults in your partner's life, but deal with your own weaknesses and your partner will often change.
- The best gift you can give your partner is a self that is emotionally whole.
- Do not enter a new relationship before you "bury" the old.
- The way you leave often determines the way you enter.
- What goes around comes around.

EPILOGUE

Looking towards the Future

Whether you've just started out in a relationship, or you have been on the same relationship journey for decades, it doesn't really matter. There will always be a need for knowledge about and investment into that relationship. Both needs *knowledge* about how the other person functions, what he/she likes and dislikes, what his/her needs are and how to communicate effectively. Concurrently it's essential to invest time meeting your partner's needs and lovingly relate to him/her. Therefore, knowledge is a key, because you can't make good decisions without it. Coupled with investment, it empowers you to avoid making simple mistakes that can cause tension in your relationship.

A relationship doesn't grow beautiful by itself; you need to sow into every relationship that you would like to be a source of happiness and joy in your life. Love and romance is a fruit that comes if you sow the right seed, tenderly take care, water and fertilize your relationship correctly. Remember, seeds are small, so try not to be overwhelmed. As you take small steps, one at the time, they will eventually grow up into something beautiful. It will never be more green and beautiful on the other side; only that side that you sow beautiful seeds and tenderly look after will be the greenest and the most beautiful. As you have come to the end of this book, and hopefully started to apply some of the principles in it, you have probably concluded that all change starts with yourself. One important thing to remember is that **each of you is ultimately responsible for your own behavior**; not your partner's. You cannot change another person, but you can change yourself and the way you respond and feel in certain situations.

We have come to the conclusion that **relationships that are happy and harmonious, filled with love and romance, are not made of individuals that all the time demand their own way**. Rather, they are made of individuals that place their partner and the partner's interests above themselves. They esteem the other better than themselves and are genuinely interested in trying to understand their partner and make him/her happy. They celebrate when their partners succeed in their ventures and they also mourn in times of loss or failure, as though their victories or losses were their own. They laugh together in times of joy and comfort one another in times of sorrow.

Let your partner know that he/she is the most important person in your life. Never take your partner for granted. Be expressive, show affection and be extravagant in your love for him/her. Never be lazy in your love for your partner. All the more, if you are married, you have given your word, or to be exact, your vows, to love for a lifetime. There was never any escape clause in your vows. Let your partner feel that he/she is the most important person in your life.

Finally, never harbor old issues in your relationship, forget those things that are behind and move towards the things ahead. Focus on and remember your relationship goals and visions that you have set up together. Your relationship will not always be a smooth ride, but if you have prepared for it, and you are well equipped, you will overcome and succeed over those obstacles in your journey. And remember, it's a journey. Enjoy it and make it pleasant.

Have a safe one and let your **Love come Ablaze**.

If you wish to have regular **relationship advice**, subscribe to our newsletter on ***relationshipaffair.com***

Andreas & Marie Skogvard

REFERENCE LIST

1. Fisher, Helen. *Anatomy of love, A Natural History of Mating, Marriage, and Why We Stray.*

   W.W Norton & Company, 2016. Used by permission of Fisher, Helen.

2. 1 Corinthians 13:4-7. Scripture quotations are taken from *The Living Bible* copyright © 1971. Used by permission of Tyndale House Publishers, Inc., Carol Stream, Illinois 60188. All rights reserved.

3. Bojanhiu, Anjeze Gonxhe. Goodreads.com. 1910-1997.

4. Britt, Sonya. *Researchers find correlations between financial arguments, decreased relationship satisfaction.* Kansas State University, July 12, 2013. Used by permission of Britt, Sonya.

5. Survey by CreditCard.com, *7.2 million Americans hiding money from spouses*, CNBC, Jan 21, 2015.

   Used by permission of Tony, Mecia (survey conductor.)

6. TD Bank's Second Annual Love and Money Survey, *TD Love and Money*, 2016:5.

7. Mehrabian, Albert. *Silent Messages: Implicit communication of emotions and attitudes.* Belmont, CA: Wadsworth, 1981:76-79. Used by permission of Mehrabian Albert.

8. Thompson, Robb. *The Ten Critical Laws of Relationship*, 2005:63.

9. Ford, Henry. *Golden wedding anniversary of Mr. and Mrs. Henry Ford will be celebrated tonight.* The Evening Independent, Apr 12, 1938.

10. Luchies, Laura. *Trust and Biased Memory of Transgressions in Romantic Relationships*, Calvin College Center for Social Research, 2013. Used by permission of Luchies, Laura.

11. 18 U.S Code, Title 18, Part I, Chapter 109A, §2246, Legal Information Institute.

12. Adler, Shannon L. *The Philosophy of Shannon L. Adler.* Used by permission of Adler, Shannon L.

13. Merriam-Webster. *The Merriam-Webster Dictionary*, 2016.

14. Cambridge English Dictionary, Cambridge University Press, 2016.

15. Nortrup, Chrisanna., Schwarz Pepper., and White James. *The Normal Bar*, 2013. Published by Harmony, an Imprint of the Crown Publishing Group, a division of Random House. Used by permission of Schwarz, Pepper.

16. Fagan, Patrick F. *The effects of Pornography on individuals, Marriage, Family and Community.* Marriage and Religion Research Institute, 2009. Used by permission of Fagan, Patrick.

17. Waldinger MD., Quinn P, Dilleen M., Mundayat R., Schweitzer DH., and Boolell M. *A multinational population survey of intravaginal ejaculation latency time.* J Sex Med. 2005 Jul: 2(4): 492-7.

18. Cole, Edwin Louis. *Strong men in tough times.* Charisma House, 1993:72.

19. Chapman, Gary. *The 5 love languages: How to Express Heartfelt Commitment to Your mate.* United States of America, 1992. Used by permission of Moody Publishers.

20. Coan, Jim. *Jim Coan and the Hand Holding Experiment.* University of Virginia.

21. Harley, Willard F. *His needs, her needs*, 2011. Questionnaire to determine a couple's needs can be downloaded free of charge at marriagebuilder.com. Used by permission of Harley Willard F.